ASIAN FUSION

ACKNOWLEDGMENTS
With many thanks to Richard S. Elman, Chairman,
Noble Group, whose generous support and trust
in my vision has made this book possible.

Special thanks to Gillian Sutch for her time, devotion and
professionalism in editing this book. Thanks, too,
Kasyan, Simon and Bryan for all their hard work and
unceasing faith in Asian Fusion, to James Smith for his
generous help in the development of this book and to
the assistance that I enjoyed in the kitchens from Papa
Chow, Thomas Tao, Richard Yeung and Dennis Tse.

Most of all, I am grateful to God for giving me the skills
to make my part in the project possible.

Dedicated to my parents Notburga and Norbert Brugger
for their faith and love.

ASIAN FUSION

WILEY

PRODUCED BY PACIFIC CENTURY PUBLISHERS LTD
SUITE 1003, KOWLOON CENTRE, 29-43 ASHLEY ROAD
TSIM SHA TSUI, KOWLOON, HONG KONG
TELEPHONE (852) 2376 2085, FAX (852) 2376 2137
COMPUSERVE 100267 2053

PRODUCER - KASYAN BARTLETT
EDITOR - GILLIAN SUTCH
DESIGN - BRYAN HOOK
PHOTOGRAPHY - SIMON WHEELER
PRODUCTION - LI SUK WOON AND TONY TANG

RECIPIES ©WINI BRUGGER
PHOTOGRAPHY ©PACIFIC CENTURY PUBLISHERS LTD
©PACIFIC CENTURY PUBLISHERS LTD

PRINTED IN CHINA

DISTRIBUTED IN THE UNITED STATES AND CANADA BY
JOHN WILEY & SONS, INC.,
605 THIRD AVENUE, NEW YORK, NY 10158-0012

LIBRARY OF CONGRESS CATALOGING-IN-PUBLICATION DATA
A CATALOGUE ENTRY FOR THIS TITLE IS AVAILABLE
FROM THE LIBRARY OF CONGRESS
ISBN 0-470-24423-2

FOREWORD BY KEN HOM

Cuisine combinations throughout the world today are mind-boggling. It is a paradox of our kitchens that, until quite recently, many of us who cook did not exploit the diversity of seasonings, spices and foods brought to the rest of the world by various different groups of Asian immigrants such as the Chinese, Japanese and Southeast Asians. Many of our dishes have remained characteristically European, heavy on meat and mildly spiced. Food preferences are so deeply rooted culturally and psychologically, the reluctance to experiment with new tastes and flavors is perhaps understandable.

Today, however, that reluctance is being overcome rapidly. The change became noticeable about twenty years ago with the emergence of such phenomena as 'la nouvelle cuisine', a style drawing upon foods and techniques once regarded as foreign or exotic. Developing at the same time, there was a growing trend which I called in the early 1980s 'East/West Cuisine' or if you wish, 'Fusion Cuisine'. It is a cooking style which emphasizes the blending of foods, spices, flavorings and techniques formerly isolated from each other within Asian or European kitchens. Its popular acceptance is no doubt related to the increasing merger of all styles - Gucci shops in Hong Kong and Chinese restaurants in Paris. But the introduction and ready acceptance of Asian influences which began in California and has now spread to other cities throughout the world such as New York, London, and Sydney, even back to Hong Kong, is due in large part perhaps to the historical immigration of Asians to Europe, America and Australia. Many of these recent arrivals have opened restaurants and food stores specializing in Asian cuisines, and featuring foods and ingredients totally unlike the chow mein or egg foo young dishes formerly offered in many cheap restaurants. In the process, they have educated and delighted the Western palate.

Coverage of the new cuisines and food combinations in cookbooks, magazines, newspapers and television programs has enhanced our understanding of and familiarity with them, and the spread of this new awareness. Specialty shops and supermarkets, responding to consumer demand, now stock foods and ingredients whose names were once found only in dictionaries. Today, such terms as stir-fry, bean curd, tofu, soya sauce, wok, sushi, fresh coriander, curry, bak choi and fresh ginger are as European as apple tart.

No one has done more to pioneer fusion cooking into a mature style than master chef Wini Brugger. His cooking does not pretend to be a new Californian, European or Franco-European cuisine. Rather it is good, honest cooking that is simple, quick, healthy and easy at the same time. Wini's fusion cooking is basically an unforced, natural blending of ingredients and techniques borrowed mainly from China, Japan, Korea, Thailand and India blended with his wide experiences of restaurant cooking and dining. He recommends local and fresh ingredients from supermarkets, but uses Asian foods and tastes with a flair that adds spice to our everyday cooking. Wini neither imitates Asian dishes, nor does he try to disguise them. As a great chef, he simply respects them while exploring their possibilities and extending their potential. He feels that a recipe is not a rigid formula but a tempting enticement to experiment. Through his imaginative recipes, it is clear that he regards cooking as an art, not a science, imitative as well as creative, experimental, imaginative and more play than work. His mouth-watering recipes are full of inspiring combinations that follow this loving playfulness and result in dishes that are both familiar and exotic, and delightfully satisfying as well. It is obvious through this bold and unique cookbook that Wini Brugger has accomplished his goal of merging cuisines and in the process he has assisted in the creation of innovative good cooking. I look forward to trying every single delicious recipe, as I know you will.

Ken Hom

Hong Kong the heart of Asia, where Asian Fusion was born.

LIFE IS FOOD AND FOOD IS LIFE

Cuisines in Asia, more than those in Europe, lend themselves to experimentation, inviting one to take an idea from one culture and blend it with an idea from another. And this concept is what I call 'Asian Fusion'. Basically, it's traditional European cooking skills challenging Asian cooking techniques and embracing and absorbing the warmth and wealth of Asian spices and seasonings.

Asian Fusion is unique, it's personal, it's simple and it's a taste intense cuisine. It's also truly contemporary and cosmopolitan, dazzling taste buds and confronting the norm. It's like fashion - you mix and match. It's like music - you don't always want to hear the same sounds - you may listen to some jazz, you may settle into a track of country or you may muse over a track of blues depending on your mood and what you want to hear. In other words it is flexible, innovative, open and tests the limits - but fundamentally it is based on a knowledge and understanding of the strengths, and weaknesses, of one's ingredients. For example, you can spark up a goulash with curry spices, but you wouldn't add soya sauce. You would tease out a fish dish with ginger or mint, but you wouldn't think of introducing it to mint jelly. It's an intensification of European cuisine, an enhancement which doesn't seem to work the other way around - I don't believe you can Europeanize Asian dishes and techniques so successfully.

Asian Fusion is also an adventure, a culinary discovery, and that is what this book is about - not designed so that you follow each recipe step by step and quantity by quantity but I'd like it to be used as an inspiration, as a guide. My hope is that it will force you to lose your inhibitions in the kitchen, for fusion allows you to make constant improvements, to experiment, to see what items you can lose and what you can add.

And how have I arrived at this culinary philosophy? Asia is home to some of the world's finest cuisines and I have been blessed to have spent the years I have in Asia working with people with strict culinary traditions but yet in a modern environment that is constantly changing. It is an eclectic environment that appeals to the adventurous chef and encourages culinary development. Ideas for dishes spring up all the time and not just for the sake of novelty but because one's surroundings and influences stretch one's repertoire, one's horizons. Fusion is not, however, confusion. More is not necessarily better, in fact sometimes less is more, and the success of this collection of recipes lies in the successful combining of select ingredients, combinations which make the results better than the traditional versions. One learns to highlight the strengths of each cuisine and side-step the weaker parts. It is also not mixing ingredients for the sake of it for fusion also means you can't necessarily do it better. If I had a beautiful piece of marguru tuna I couldn't do anything to improve on it in any way other than to serve it in traditional fashion, as sashimi. What I could do, however, is serve it with grilled vegetables and a salad to make a more substantial dish. And this is the essence of Asian Fusion - judgement is all important as to what can be fused and what can't. And to know what will and what won't is a matter of practice, experience and a dash of spontaneity. Above all, you need to be your own worst critic.

Wini Brugger

CHEF'S STORY - WINI BRUGGER

Wini Brugger's earliest ambition was to be either a musician, an actor or a chef. His family's intention, however, was that he pursue a more 'responsible' career, preferably in one of the professions. By age 14 Wini had chosen, with typical unswerving decisiveness, to become a chef.

He began the long training with a three-year apprenticeship in Austria's highest village, Heiligenblut, at the Glockner-Hof. Cooking was everything he wanted, and he soon distinguished himself. The internationally renowned Austrian chef, Werner Matt, accepted him as a chef, and Wini spent two years under Matt's tutelage. "He was a tough task master," Wini recalls, "but that training brought out the best in me. I was forced to start from basics, chopping vegetables and making sauces. That background has been invaluable; I consider it my making."

Mastering classic French cuisine was the next challenge as he took up a post at Le Richemond Hotel in Geneva, a period during which he also learned to speak excellent French. Wini then went to the Tel Aviv Hilton with the assignment of opening the King Solomon Grill. Cooking according to kosher requirements - preparing food without cream, butter, or alcohol, the very staples of French cuisine - expanded his repertoire in yet another direction.

Seeking new challenges, Wini moved to the Hilton's Drake Hotel in Chicago. From there it was an easy move to Hong Kong to join the Hong Kong Hilton team initially as Sous Chef. Then, as Chef of The Grill, he won acclaim for his innovative cooking style and, three years later, became Executive Chef. In this role, Wini oversaw 170 chefs working in nine restaurants catering to local as well as international guests. The triumph of the Hilton team at the Culinary Olympics testifies to his skill as a team leader. In early 1994, Wini was promoted to the position of Regional Executive Chef for Central Asia. For Wini, working in Asia has been exhilarating. "Sometimes the time is right, and for me that happened when I arrived in Hong Kong. I had the technical ability, but in previous jobs lacked the chance to express my individuality. Hong Kong has allowed me to get on with what I want to do: to explore, experiment, and create beyond the usual bounds."

Much of Wini's success as a chef derives from his inquisitive nature. Asian cuisine and its chefs have been a constant source of challenge and inspiration. "How can one improve on traditional cuisine, like Japanese, Chinese, French? The answer is you cannot. But, if you match the weaknesses and strengths of different cuisines, you can come up with something truly great."

In 1993 Wini and two other Hilton chefs, produced a stunning cookbook 'The Cutting Edge', a forerunner of 'Asian Fusion'.

On May 1st, 1995, Wini started his own company, WB International Ltd., a culinary multi-media business specializing in restaurant software, gourmet foods, promotions, restaurant consultancy and television. His TV series 'Wild Ginger' was a big success in Asia. For someone less daring, leaving an established career might have seemed a foolhardy proposition. Yet Wini has never been one to shy away from a challenge. As his favourite author, Goethe, once wrote: "Whatever you can do, or dream you can, begin it. Boldness has genius, power and magic in it." Had Goethe lived to meet Wini, he might have amended that to say genius also has boldness in it.

SALADS/STARTERS

All recipes serve four people

CHILI FLAKE POTATO SALAD WITH TURMERIC CHICKEN AND MIHUNA LEAVES

INGREDIENTS

4 small chicken breasts, 1 cup firmly packed fresh mihuna leaves* (or spinach), 1/4 lb goose liver, 1/2 tsp paprika, 2 tsps turmeric, 1 egg white, 2 tsps light soya sauce, 1/2 cup white breadcrumbs, 1/2 lb butter.

For the potato salad: 1/2 lb new potatoes in their jackets, 1 tsp mustard, 1 cup warm chicken broth, 2 tsps low-fat mayonnaise, 4 chopped shallots, 2 tsps chili flakes, 2 tsps shredded cilantro leaves, salt and pepper.

Garnish: 1 sliced yellow bell pepper, 1 finely chopped green onion, 1 tsp chili flakes.

METHOD

1 Cut the chicken breasts open and flatten.
2 Wash the mihuna (or spinach) leaves. Lay out leaves on dry kitchen towel.
3 Slice the raw goose liver and arrange it on top of the mihuna. Wrap up into 4 individual parcels.
4 Place a goose liver parcel inside each chicken breast and fold chicken breasts up tightly.
5 Season the breasts with paprika and turmeric, brush with the egg white and soya sauce and coat with the breadcrumbs.
6 Slowly fry the stuffed breasts in butter until golden brown. Keep warm until ready to serve.
7 Steam or boil the potatoes and when cooked, peel and cut into wedges.
8 Combine the mustard, broth, mayonnaise, shallots, chili flakes and cilantro with salt and pepper to taste. Toss this dressing with the potato wedges.
9 Saute the yellow bell pepper and green onion quickly over high heat.
10 Arrange a portion of potato salad on each plate, cut the breasts in half to reveal stuffing. Garnish with the bell pepper and green onion.

* available from Japanese stores.

ASIAN FUSION **SALADS/STARTERS**

LAMB CARPACCIO WITH MUSTARD, CURRY AND CRUSHED PEPPER

INGREDIENTS

3/4 lb raw lamb fillet, 12 morel mushrooms, 1 tbsp butter, 1 tsp chopped garlic, 2 chopped shallots.
For the dressing: 2 tsps olive oil, 2 tsps mild curry powder, 1 tsp crushed black pepper, 2 tsps mild prepared mustard, 2 tsps chopped parsley. **For the salad:** 4 romaine lettuce leaves, 4 celery stems.
Garnish: 4 tbsps curry mayonnaise (recipe below), 1/4 cup fresh Parmesan shavings, freshly crushed black pepper.

METHOD

1   Deep-freeze lamb for one day. Slice paper thin, ideally with a meat slicer.
2   Transfer slices to serving plates.
3   Combine the dressing ingredients and brush on top of the sliced meat.
4   Soak morels in salted water overnight and clean them of any sand or dirt. Saute quickly in garlic and shallots. Keep warm.
5   Decorate the plates with curry mayonnaise as in the picture. Garnish with salad leaves, top with Parmesan shavings and crushed black pepper.

CURRY MAYONNAISE

INGREDIENTS

1 egg yolk, 1 tbsp mild Sri Lankan curry powder, 2 tbsps white wine, juice of 1/2 lemon, salt and pepper, 1/2 cup olive oil.

METHOD

1   Put the egg yolk in a blender.
2   Add remaining ingredients, except the oil. Blend.
3   Slowly add the oil until thick and creamy.

HOT JAPANESE VERMICELLI AND CUCUMBER SALAD WITH SAKE GLAZED LOBSTER

SEE PAGE 18

INGREDIENTS

1 lobster, 1 cup dry vermicelli or bean thread noodles, 1 medium cucumber.
For the marinade: 9 tbsps virgin olive oil, 2 tbsps sake, 5 tsps rice wine vinegar, 1 tsp chili flakes, 4 tsps sugar, 2 tsps soya sauce, 1/2 tsp wasabi, 1 tsp salt, 1 tsp Japanese red pepper. For the salad: 1/2 cup yellow fungus, 1/2 cup green Japanese seaweed, 1/2 cup frisee salad hearts, 1 cup firmly packed bak choi leaves.
Garnish: 1 tbsp thinly sliced green onions, 1 1/2 tsps toasted sesame seeds.

METHOD

1 Combine the marinade ingredients which will be used for both the lobster and the noodles.
2 Blanch the lobster for 6 minutes. Remove the meat from the shell and chop into small pieces.
   Toss the lobster with a few spoonfuls of the marinade. Keep warm.
3. Blanch the vermicelli or bean thread noodles in boiling water until just tender. Drain and transfer to a bowl and toss with 2/3 of the remaining marinade.
4 Peel and seed the cucumber. Cut into quarters lengthwise and then into thin strips.
5 Mix lobster and noodles with cucumber. Add the fungus and salad leaves. Toss with remainder of marinade, place on plates and serve immediately.

BRONZE FENNEL FLAVORED MACKEREL WITH WATER-CRESS AND SATSUMA SALAD

SEE PAGE 19

INGREDIENTS

1/2 lb fresh mackerel fillets. For the salad: 2 - 3 bulbs fresh bronze fennel with leaves, 12 shiitake mushrooms, 2 satsumas, separated into segments, 1/2 lb watercress, 1 sliced red bell pepper, 2 tsps freshly chopped tarragon.
For the salad dressing: juice of 1 satsuma, 3 tsps olive oil, 4 tsps rice wine vinegar, salt and pepper.

METHOD

1 Finely slice the fennel bulbs and toss with the shiitake and satsuma segments. Reserve the leaves. In a separate bowl toss the watercress with the bell pepper slices and tarragon.
2 Combine the salad dressing and pour equally over the two salad mixtures.
3 Grill the mackerel fillets gently on a strip of bronze fennel leaves until well done.
4 Arrange the fennel and shiitake mushrooms with the satsuma salad on the plates, top with the hot fish and serve the watercress and bell pepper salad to the side.

AHI TUNA SASHIMI STRIPS WITH MIZUNA AND AVOCADO

SEE PAGE 20

INGREDIENTS

1/4 lb raw tuna, 6 quail eggs, 2 avocados.

For the salad: 1/2 lb mizuna greens, 1 cup firmly packed fresh spinach, 1/2 cup diced tomato, 1/2 cup sliced carrots, 2 tbsps pickled ginger.

For the dressing: 2 tsps balsamic vinegar, 4 tsps olive oil, 1 chopped shallot, 1 tbsp chopped chives, 1/2 tsp shano pepper*, 2 tsps Japanese soya sauce.

1 Cut the tuna into thin strips.
2 Cook the quail eggs in slightly salted water for approximately 1 1/2 minutes. Chill in cold water, shell and cut in half.
3 Rinse and drain the mizuna and spinach. Mix with the tomato, carrot and pickled ginger.
4 Combine the dressing ingredients and toss with the salad and the tuna.
5 Cut avocados in half, remove the pit and slice.
6 Place tossed salad onto the plates, garnish with sliced avocado and 1 1/2 quail eggs.

*available from Japanese stores

BARBECUED BABY PORK WITH CURRIED BEAN SALAD

SEE PAGE 21

INGREDIENTS

1/4 lb diced barbecued baby pork*.

For the bean salad: 1/2 lb dry white beans, 5 bay leaves, 2 tbsps fresh sage, 1/4 cup finely diced carrots, 1/4 cup finely diced celery, 1/4 cup seeded and diced tomato, 2 tsps chopped parsley. **For the salad:** 1/2 lb young spinach leaves, 1/4 lb radicchio. **For the dressing:** 1 cup virgin olive oil, 4 tbsps sherry vinegar, 2 tbsps lemon juice, 1/2 tsp Dijon mustard, 1 tsp Indian curry powder, 1 tbsp chutney, 1 tsp freshly minced garlic, salt and pepper. **Garnish according to taste:** garlic chive stems, shredded carrot, crispy pork skin, 1 shallot, quartered.

METHOD

1 Sort and rinse the beans, then soak overnight. Next morning, drain.
2 Put the beans in 8 cups of water with the bay leaves and sage. Bring to the boil and simmer for about 40 minutes, until tender. Remove the bay leaves and drain the beans.
3 Whilst the beans are cooking, mix the carrots (reserving some for the garnish), celery, tomato and parsley together. Add the diced pork.
4 Combine the dressing ingredients and pour over vegetable mixture. Add the beans and toss well. Season with the salt and pepper.
5 Decorate the plates with the spinach and radicchio, pile on the bean salad and garnish with garlic chive stems, shredded carrot, crispy pork skin and quartered shallot.

*Barbecued pork can be bought from many Chinese roast goods store or from restaurants. You can also make it at home: the recipe is on page 32.

BLACK BEAN SALAD WITH CRISPY SESAME CRAB CLAW

SEE PAGE 22

INGREDIENTS

For the bean salad: 1/2 lb dry black beans, 1 lemon grass stalk broken in half, 1/2 cup finely diced red onion, 1/2 cup finely diced red bell pepper.
For the salad: 1/2 lb julienne of salad leaves (romaine, butter and radicchio lettuces).
For the salad dressing: 2 tbsps freshly chopped cilantro, 1/2 tsp ground cumin, 4 tsps olive oil, 1 - 2 tbsps rice wine vinegar, cayenne pepper to taste, 1 tsp minced garlic, 2 tsps tomato paste.
For the crab claws: 4 crab claws, 1 cup chicken mousse (see right), 1 egg white, 1/4 cup white breadcrumbs, 2 tsps ground sesame seed, 1 cup olive oil, 3 tsps sesame oil. Garnish: 1/2 lb enoki mushrooms.

METHOD

1   Sort, rinse and soak the beans overnight. Drain, then rinse again.
2. Put the beans in 4 1/2 cups water with the lemon grass and bring to the boil. Reduce heat and simmer until tender - between 30 - 45 minutes. Drain, discard the lemon grass.
3   Toss beans with the onion and pepper.
4   Combine ingredients for the dressing - except the tomato paste. Mix half with the beans, and half with the julienned greens. Season to taste. Add 1 tsp of tomato paste to the bean mixture and 1 tsp to the greens. Toss.
5   Cook the crab claws.
6   Coat the claws with chicken mousse and brush the meat with egg white. Mix breadcrumbs and ground sesame seeds together and dip claws into the mixture, coating thickly.
7   Deep fry the claws in olive and sesame oil until golden brown.
8   Blanch enoki mushrooms for 1 minute.
9   Serve claws on the beans and salad leaves. Garnish with enoki mushrooms. Accompany with chili sauce.

TANGERINE CRAB MEAT SALAD ON A BED OF MARINATED TOMATO

SEE PAGE 23

INGREDIENTS

3/4 lb freshly cooked crab meat, juice of 2 tangerines, 1/2 lb plum tomatoes.
For the tomato dressing: 1/4 cup diced sun-dried tomatoes, juice of 1/2 lemon, 1 tsp shredded basil, 2 chopped shallots. For the salad: 1/2 lb mache salad.
For the salad dressing: 3 tbsps olive oil, 1/4 tbsp sesame oil, 2 tsps shredded cilantro leaves, 1 tsp balsamic vinegar. Garnish: 1 cup vermicelli.

METHOD

1   Marinate crab meat in the tangerine juice for 15 minutes. Chill.
2   Combine the ingredients for the tomato dressing.
3   Peel and quarter the tomatoes and marinate in the dressing for 30 minutes.
4   Combine the ingredients for the salad dressing and toss with the mache salad.
5   Deep fry the vermicelli.
6   Arrange the tomato quarters around the edge of the plates. Place the mache salad on the side and finish off with the tangerine flavoured crab meat topped with deep fried vermicelli.

CHICKEN MOUSSE

INGREDIENTS

1 chicken breast, minced, 1 cup cream, 1 egg, salt, 1 tbsp chopped cilantro, 1 tbsp chopped basil, 1 tbsp soya sauce.

METHOD

1   Blend chicken slowly with the cream.
2   Add the egg and season.
3   Add chopped herbs and soya sauce.
4   Put through a sieve and chill until ready to use.

STIR FRIED ENDIVE SALAD WITH RIVER CRAYFISH

SEE PAGE 24

INGREDIENTS

1 1/4 lb fresh river crayfish in the shell, juice of
1 kaffir lime, 1 tbsp chopped basil, 1/2 tsp prepared
mustard, 1/2 tsp minced fresh garlic, 1/2 lb chopped
button mushrooms. **For the salad:** 4 endive, 1 cup
tightly packed green mustard leaf, 1 tsp sesame oil,
3 tsps balsamic vinegar.
For the crayfish sauce: crayfish shells (especially the
heads), 3 tsps olive oil, 1 tsp sesame oil, 1/2 cup diced
carrot, 1/2 cup diced tomato, 3 Thai lemon leaves, 2 tsps
cilantro leaves, salt and pepper, 1 tbsp tomato paste,
2 tbsps rice wine vinegar, 4 cups chicken stock, 1 tsp
cornstarch. **Garnish:** 2 tsps Asian pesto (recipe page 61).

METHOD

1   Parboil the crayfish for 5 minutes. Remove, cool
    briefly and extract meat. Reserve shells. Keep the
    tails warm.
2   Combine the kaffir lime juice, basil, mustard and
    garlic and toss with the cooked crayfish tails.
3   Saute the shells in a mixture of olive oil and sesame
    oil. Add carrot, tomato, lemon leaves, cilantro and
    salt and pepper and saute until the vegetables
    soften. Add tomato paste and deglaze with the rice
    wine vinegar. Add the chicken stock, partially cover
    the pot and simmer for about 30 minutes. Strain and
    reduce the liquid by half. Bind with cornstarch mixed
    with a little water to make a thin sauce, and season.
4   Add half the crayfish sauce to the crayfish tails.
5   Cut endive in half and shred mustard leaves.
    Mix with the chopped mushroom.
6   Saute the endive, mustard leaf and mushrooms
    and mix in a few drops of sesame oil with the
    balsamic vinegar and a few drops of the crayfish
    sauce. This will take only a few seconds. The purpose
    is to give the salad warmth, without cooking it.
6   Arrange a serving of the endive salad in the centre of
    each plate. Place the crayfish on top.
7   Decorate the plate with small dollops of pesto.

WASABI INFUSED TARTAR OF SALMON AND SCALLOPS WITH PICKLED GINGER

SEE PAGE 25

INGREDIENTS

3/4 lb raw salmon, juice of 1/2 lemon, 1 tsp white wine,
1/2 tsp olive oil, 4 tsps tomato catsup, fresh dill and
basil, 1 tsp wasabi, 1/2 tsp pickled ginger, 1/2 cup
chopped scallops*.**For the salad:** 1/2 lb brown frisee
salad (or any other strong flavored salad greens),
6 tbsps olive oil, 3 tbsps herb vinegar.
Garnish: 1 thinly sliced cucumber, 4 tbsps sour cream,
1 tsp caviar, pinch saffron threads, 3/4 cup chicken stock.

SPECIAL EQUIPMENT

4" metal pastry ring

METHOD

1   Mince the salmon finely.
2   Combine the lemon juice, white wine, olive oil,
    catsup, fresh herbs, wasabi and ginger. Season to
    taste. Mix half the marinade with the salmon and
    place in the fridge for 10 - 15 minutes.
3   Chop the scallops finely and marinate in the
    remaining marinade.
4   Mix the dressing and toss with the salad greens.
5   Place the ring in the centre of a serving plate. Fill 1/2
    the ring with 1/4 of the salmon tartar, press firmly so
    the tartar will hold its shape when the ring is removed.
6   Fill the remaining half with the scallop tartar.
7   Remove the ring when pressed into shape.
    Repeat the procedure on the other three plates.
8   Arrange the cucumber slices in a ring around the
    salmon and scallop mixture. Place the salad greens
    and herbs around the plate and decorate the rings
    with a spoonful of sour cream.
9   Put the saffron into the chicken stock. Bring to the
    boil and simmer for a few minutes. Remove from the
    heat and allow to infuse.
10 Dribble the saffron jus over the salad.
11 Decorate with the caviar.

*If the scallops are not 100% fresh you may prefer to
steam them until well done and then chop them.

BARBECUED PORK

SEE PAGE 21

INGREDIENTS

8 lbs lean pork. **For the boiling sauce:** 3/4 lb Chinese seafood sauce*, 3/4 lb bean paste, 3/4 lb sesame paste, 1/2 lb artificial sweetener. **For the marinade:** 1/2 lb sugar, 1/4 cup salt, 1/4 bottle light soya sauce, 1/4 bottle Chinese rose wine*, 1/2 lb tomato paste.
For basting: 1 1/2 lbs malt sugar, 2 cups water.

METHOD

1   Divide pork into 3 equal pieces.
2   Combine ingredients for boiling sauce and bring to the boil. Simmer gently to allow flavors to develop and then set aside to cool.
3   When cool, add the marinade ingredients and when thoroughly mixed add the pork. Leave to marinate for an hour.
4   Meanwhile, mix the malt sugar with 2 cups of water.
5   Cook the pork either in an oven, barbecue or grill for 30 - 40 minutes until cooked.
6   As soon as the pork is removed from the heat, brush the pieces generously with the malt sugar solution. Allow to cool before eating.

*available from Chinese stores

SOUPS

All recipes serve four people

JAPANESE BEEF UDON NOODLE SOUP

INGREDIENTS

1/2 lb saruki udon (frozen)*, 1 lb US beef, sliced paper thin, 1/2 cup enoki mushrooms, 1 1/2 cups soup stock.

For the soup stock: 2 1/2 cups water, 1 cup light soya sauce (usukuchi), 1 cup sweet wine, 1/2 cup shredded green onion, 3 tbsps salty fish (nihonshi), 2 tbsps ground poy mushroom powder, 1/4 cup bonito shavings (katsuobushi).

Garnish: 1 sliced green onion, 1/2 tsp Japanese pepper sashimi.

METHOD

1   Combine soup stock ingredients and leave overnight in the fridge. Next day, bring to the boil, lower heat and simmer for 15 minutes. Cool, strain and season to taste.

2   Blanch the noodles, drain.

3   Heat the soup stock. Add the udon noodles and then the enoki mushrooms. When they are heated through remove them from the stock and transfer to serving bowls. Arrange some sliced beef on the top and pour the hot soup over.

4   Garnish with the sliced green onion and Japanese pepper sashimi.

*available from Japanese stores, as are the other Japanese items.

GRILLED SHIITAKE MUSHROOM CAPPUCCINO WITH CHILI POWDER

INGREDIENTS
1/2 lb sliced shiitake mushrooms, 1/2 tsp sesame oil, 4 cups chicken stock, 2 chopped shallots, 1 tsp minced garlic, 1 tsp shredded basil, 1/2 tsp chili powder, 1 cup skim milk. **Garnish:** 1 tsp shredded chives.

SPECIAL UTENSILS
Cappuccino maker

METHOD
1   Grill the shiitake mushrooms with sesame oil.
2   Bring the broth to a boil. Add the mushrooms and simmer for 15 minutes.
3   Saute the shallots and garlic. Add basil and chili powder. Puree in a blender and season to taste.
4   Warm the skim milk and, using a cappuccino maker, blow in hot air.
5   Ladle the hot soup into bowls. Top with the foamy milk.
6   Sprinkle with chives and serve immediately.

CHICKEN STOCK

INGREDIENTS
1 chicken, 6 cups water, 2 carrots, 1 leek, 1 onion, 1 clove garlic, 1 tbsp chopped parsley, 1 tbsp chopped cilantro leaves, 1 tbsp dry mushroom powder, salt.

METHOD
1   Wash and dice the chicken, leaving the breasts intact.
2   Wash and dice the vegetables.
3   Put chicken and vegetables into a pan and pour on cold water.
4   Slowly bring to the boil, add mushroom powder and salt and simmer for one hour.
5   Remove the breasts after 20 minutes and use in a salad.
6   Strain stock and cool.

The Chinese make chicken stock with a whole chicken - flesh, bones and all, whereas Europeans tend to use just the bones. The better the stock, the better the soup and the more flesh and bones that have been incorporated, the better the result. It is advisable, when making stock, to make more than is needed for a particular dish because if you have more liquid you can reduce and concentrate the flavors better, plus additional stock can be frozen and used in other recipes.

GREEN TEA SOUP WITH CHRYSANTHEMUM PETALS

SEE PAGE 36

INGREDIENTS

For the Asian vegetable stock: 8 cups water, 2 diced onions, 3/4 cup diced carrots, 3/4 cup diced celery, 3/4 cup diced tomato, 1 cup firmly packed red spinach, 2 tsps minced garlic, 1 tsp minced ginger, 2 tsps cilantro leaves, 2 oz sliced shiitake mushrooms, 2 tsps ginseng powder, salt and pepper. **For the soup:** 8 heads of bak choi, 3/4 lb Japanese noodles, 1 tbsp green tea powder, 1 tbsp chrysanthemum petals, 1 tbsp mild chili flakes.

METHOD

1 Boil the water, add all the stock ingredients and simmer for 1 - 1 1/2 hours. Strain.
2 Add the bak choi and when done, add the noodles and continue to simmer for 2 minutes.
3 Add the green tea powder and chrysanthemum petals. Season to taste with salt and pepper.
4 Sprinkle with chili flakes.

LEMON LEAF BISQUE WITH POTATO MATCHSTICKS

SEE PAGE 37

INGREDIENTS

For the soup: 1 cup young leeks, 3/4 lb potatoes, 1 minced onion, 1 - 2 tsps soya sauce, 3 tbsps olive oil, 1 tsp minced garlic, 4 cups chicken stock, 3 tsps red wine vinegar, 1 tbsp sliced green onion, 8 Vietnamese lemon leaves, 1 sprig fresh rosemary. **Garnish:** 1 tbsp lemon olive oil, 4 sprigs rosemary, 8 lemon leaves.

METHOD

1 Wash the leeks, especially at the base, then slice.
2 Peel the potatoes and divide in half. Put half to one side for use as garnish and cube the remainder.
3 Saute the onion and soya sauce in the olive oil and when soft add the leek slices and potato cubes. Add the garlic, then the stock and red wine vinegar, and finally the green onion, lemon leaves and rosemary. Simmer for 1 hour.
4 Puree in a blender, strain and return to the saucepan to heat through. Season to taste with salt and pepper.
5 Cut reserved potato into matchsticks and deep fry in vegetable oil until crisp. Drain on kitchen towel and season with salt.
6 Serve soup with a few drops of lemon olive oil, potato matchsticks, rosemary sprigs and lemon leaves.

VIETNAMESE BASIL SOUP WITH LETTUCE AND PRAWNS

SEE PAGE 38

INGREDIENTS

8 large prawns, 3 oz (dry) rice noodles.

For the soup: 4 1/2 cups chicken stock, 1 tsp minced fresh garlic, 1 tsp minced ginger, 2 tsps oyster sauce, 8 tsps soya sauce, 1/2 cup finely sliced carrot, 4 stalks bak choi chopped into 1 - 1 1/2" pieces, 10 small hearts of romaine lettuce, 1/2 cup mung bean sprouts, 1 tbsp shredded fresh Vietnamese basil.

METHOD

1   Shell and de-vein the prawns. Reserve for cooking at the last minute.
2   Blanch the rice noodles in boiling water to soften, drain.
3   Bring the chicken stock to the boil. Add the garlic, ginger, oyster and soya sauces. Add the carrots, bak choi, half the lettuce, the sprouts and the basil.
4   When ready to serve, add the prawns and cook for 1 minute. Serve garnished with the remaining lettuce.

ROASTED SCALLOP AND CURRY SOUP WITH STICKY RICE

SEE PAGE 39

INGREDIENTS

1/2 lb fresh scallops, 1 tsp butter, 1/4 cup glutinous rice, 1 tsp red wine vinegar, 1 tsp oyster sauce.

For the soup: 1 tsp butter, 1 chopped shallot, 2 tsps Sri Lankan curry powder, 5 cups chicken stock, 1 stalk of lemon grass, 1 cup coconut milk, juice and zest of 2 kaffir limes, salt and pepper.

METHOD

1   Slice the scallops and saute half of them quickly over a very high heat until just cooked. Half will be used for the soup, half for the garnish.
2   Saute the shallot in the butter until golden brown. Add the curry powder and continue to cook for 1 - 2 minutes.
3   Add the stock. Simmer partially covered for 10 minutes.
4   Add the lemon grass and cook for another 20 minutes. Remove the lemon grass, add the sauteed scallops and puree in a blender together with the coconut milk and kaffir lime juice until smooth (or coarse, if preferred). Season with salt and pepper.
5   Dip remaining scallops (2 - 3 per person) in a little cornstarch and lightly pan fry in oil on both sides. Add a few drops of wine vinegar together with the oyster sauce to coat scallops. Remove immediately.
6   Steam glutinous rice until cooked.
7   Put a couple of spoonfuls of sticky rice in each bowl, pour soup around and garnish with roasted scallops and kaffir lime zest.

GINGERED TOMATO BROTH WITH CELERY LEAVES

SEE PAGE 40

INGREDIENTS

For the broth: 4 lbs chopped veal shank, 8 cups water, 1/4 cup sliced carrots, 1 sliced onion, 1 tsp celery seeds, 2 tsps thyme, 1 tsp minced garlic, 1/4 cup dried shiitake mushrooms, 2 tsps dried scallops, 8 lemon leaves, 1 tsp shredded cilantro, 2 tsps fresh diced tomato, salt and pepper. For the soup: 2 large tomatoes, 2 cups tomato juice, 4 cups broth (as per the above), 1 cup vermicelli, 2 tsps finely minced fresh ginger, 3 tsps chopped basil, 1/2 tsp minced fresh garlic. Garnish: 8 yellow celery leaves, 2 diced tomatoes.

METHOD

1   Combine the ingredients for the broth, bring to the boil and simmer for 1 1/2 hours. Strain and season with salt and pepper.
2   Seed and dice the fresh tomatoes. Bring the tomato juice and broth to the boil and add the diced tomato.
3   Add the vermicelli and cook for another 4 minutes.
4   Add the ginger, basil and garlic and adjust seasoning with salt and pepper.
5   Serve garnished with celery leaves and diced tomato.

DHAL SOUP WITH BARLEY AND SHISO TEMPURA

SEE PAGE 41

INGREDIENTS

1/4 cup lentils, 1/4 cup barley, 8 cups chicken stock, 1/4 cup green Thai curry powder, 3 tsps shredded basil, 1/4 cup diced carrots, 1/4 cup sliced celery, 1/4 cup diced tomatoes, 3 tsps basil, salt, freshly ground black pepper. Garnish: Ready-made tempura batter mix*, 8 shiso leaves, 4 quartered, skinned and de-seeded tomatoes, 4 chives.

METHOD

1   Soak lentils overnight, then steam for 20 minutes.
2   Soak the barley for an hour.
3   Combine the stock and green curry powder. Bring to the boil, add the steamed lentils and soaked barley. Simmer for 20 minutes.
4   Add the basil, carrots, celery and diced tomatoes to the soup.
5   Mix tempura powder with water or beer. Dip the shiso leaves into this batter and quickly deep-fry in vegetable oil. Dry well on kitchen towel.
6   Season soup with salt and pepper, garnish with tempura shiso leaves and tomato quarters tied up in a chive string.

* available from Japanese stores.

PASTA

All recipes serve four people

TAGLIATELLE WITH SPICY SZECHUAN SAUCE AND TEPPANYAKI SIRLOIN

INGREDIENTS

1/2 lb tagliatelle (dry), 1 cup cooked kidney beans, 1/2 lb beef sirloin, 2 tbsps light sesame oil, 1 tsp crushed black pepper.

For the sauce: 3 tbsps chopped onion, 1/2 cup diced bell pepper, 1 cup red wine, 3/4 cup canned tomatoes, 1 tsp minced fresh garlic, 1/2 tsp chopped fresh ginger, 1 tsp cilantro leaves, 1/2 tsp cayenne pepper, 1 tsp rice wine vinegar, 3 tbsps hot chili sauce.

METHOD

1   To make the sauce, braise the onion and bell pepper in the red wine until soft.
2   Puree the tomatoes and add to the wine mixture, together with the garlic, ginger, cilantro leaves, cayenne pepper, rice wine vinegar and chili sauce. Simmer gently for 15 - 20 minutes until flavors are well blended.
3   Add kidney beans and season to taste.
4   Thickly coat the sirloin with crushed black pepper and a bit of sesame oil. Cook on a flat top grill, or in a non-stick pan, until medium rare.
5   Cook the tagliatelle in boiling (unsalted) water to which 1 tsp of oil has been added until 'al dente'. Drain.
6   Mix the pasta with the bean sauce.
7   Place pasta and bean sauce onto the plates and top with sliced sirloin.

CILANTRO SEED PASTA WITH SOYA YOGHURT

INGREDIENTS

1/2 lb cilantro seed pasta (recipe follows), 2 sliced shallots, 1 tbsp butter, 1 tsp minced garlic, 1 cup sliced mixed Asian and European mushrooms, 1/4 cup bean sprouts, 8 tbsps cooked green peas, 1 tsp chopped fresh cilantro, 3 tbsps white wine, salt and pepper, 1 tsp chili powder, 1 egg, 3 tbsps yoghurt, 1/4 cup diced tomato, 4 tbsps soya sauce.

METHOD

1   Cook the pasta in boiling water until 'al dente' - approximately 3 minutes. Drain, cool.
2   Saute the shallots in the butter. Add the garlic and mushrooms.
3   When fragrant add the bean sprouts.
4   When these are nearly done, add the peas, cilantro and wine. Season to taste with salt, pepper and chili powder.
5   Beat the egg slightly. Fold in the yoghurt, the diced tomato and the soya sauce.
6   Put the vegetables and pasta in an oven-proof dish, cover with the soya yoghurt and bake in a pre-heated oven - gas mark 4, 350˚F for 5 minutes until brown.

CILANTRO SEED PASTA

INGREDIENTS

5 eggs, 1/2 lb flour, 1/4 cup finely crushed cilantro seeds, 1/2 tsp sesame oil, 1 tsp olive oil, 1 cup warm water, salt and pepper, 1 tsp cornmeal.

Blend all the ingredients together to make a firm dough. Work quickly and when firm allow to rest for 1 hour. Use a pasta maker if you have one to make fettucine. If not, roll out the dough on a clean work surface to a thinness of 1/8". Allow to rest again for 2 hours in order to dry and become more workable. Using a ruler, cut strips 1/2" x 6". Brush lightly with cornmeal and boil in water for 3 - 4 minutes until 'al dente'.

BUCKWHEAT NOODLES WITH BAK CHOI AND FRIED WILD GARLIC

SEE PAGE 50

INGREDIENTS

1/2 lb buckwheat noodles (soba), 1 tsp minced fresh wild garlic, 1/4 cup kim chee. **For the vegetables:**
2 1/4 cups chicken stock, 1 cup sliced onion, 1 tsp minced fresh ginger, 1 cup diced carrots, 1 cup finely sliced cabbage, 1 cup baby bak choi, 2 tsps cornstarch, 2 tsps soya sauce, 1 tsp red wine vinegar.

1 Bring a pan of salted water to the boil and plunge in the soba for 30 seconds. Remove, drain and keep warm.
2 To cook the vegetables, bring the chicken stock to a boil and braise onion and ginger for 3 - 4 minutes.
3 Add the carrots, cabbage and bak choi and continue to simmer for 5 minutes. Put 4 bak choi leaves aside for garnish.
4 Fry the wild garlic in vegetable oil until golden brown. Remove and dry on a paper kitchen towel.
5 Combine the cornstarch, soya sauce and vinegar. Stir into the simmering vegetables and continue to cook - and stir - for another 1 - 2 minutes until the sauce has thickened.
6 Add the kim chee to the simmering vegetables and finish off with the fried garlic.
7 Place vegetable mixture on plates, top with soba noodles and garnish with bak choi leaves.

BLACK PEPPER LINGUINI WITH RED TOMATO SAUCE AND BAK CHOI STEMS

SEE PAGE 51

INGREDIENTS

1 lb 5 oz linguini, 10 bak choi stems.
For the sauce: 14 peeled, seeded and chopped plum tomatoes, 8 chopped garlic cloves, 1 chopped onion, 1 tsp balsamic vinegar, 1 tsp caster sugar, 1/4 tsp chili flakes, 1 tsp fresh shredded basil, 1 tsp fresh chopped parsley, 1/2 tsp black pepper, salt to taste.

METHOD

1 Place the plum tomatoes, garlic and onion in a blender and process until smooth.
2 Add the vinegar, sugar, chili flakes, basil, parsley and black pepper and bring to the boil. Cook for 5 minutes. Season with salt. Keep warm.
3 Steam bak choi stems, slice and keep warm.
4 Cook the linguini in a large pot of water with a teaspoon of oil in it until 'al dente'.
5 Drain, toss whilst still warm with the sauce and sliced bak choi slices.

SIAMESE TOMATO RISOTTO WITH SAFFRON MULLET

SEE PAGE 52

INGREDIENTS

For the fish: 4 red mullet fillets, 1 tsp saffron threads, 2 tbsps olive oil, salt and pepper.

For the risotto: 1 tsp minced fresh garlic, 2 cups tom yam goong stock, 1 cup arborio rice, 1 cup tomato juice, 1 cup sliced mushrooms, 1/2 tsp Thai curry powder, 1 tsp basil, 2 tbsps butter, 1/2 cup chopped tomato. Garnish: coarsely ground black pepper.

METHOD

1　Mix the saffron and olive oil, season with salt and pepper and marinate the mullet fillets, at room temperature, for 5 - 10 minutes. Pan fry until golden brown.

2　In a deep saucepan, gently fry the garlic and when soft add 2 tbsps of stock. Heat and then add the rice and a further cup of stock. Bring to the boil, then reduce the heat and simmer gently, uncovered, for 10 minutes. Stir occasionally.

3　Add the rest of the stock and bring to the boil.

4　When most of the liquid has evaporated, add the tomato juice, mushrooms, curry powder and basil. Cook for 10 minutes.

5　Stir in the butter and the chopped tomato. The rice should be moist.

6　Place the risotto on the plates, top with the red mullet, and finish with crushed black pepper.

THAI ZUCCHINI LASAGNE WITH KAFFIR LIME

SEE PAGE 53

INGREDIENTS

1/2 lb spinach lasagne sheets, 4 medium size zucchini.

For the sauce: 2 1/2 cups chopped onions, 1 cup red wine, 1 tsp garlic, 1/2 tbsp Thai red curry paste, 1/2 cup dessicated coconut, juice of 2 kaffir limes, 2 tsps fresh cilantro leaves, 1 tsp chopped parsley, salt and ground Thai green peppercorns, 20 canned tomatoes.

For garnish: shavings of Parmesan cheese, Asian pesto (see page 61).

METHOD

1　Blanch the lasagne sheets to soften.

2　Slice the zucchini lengthwise into 1" thick slices. Blanch and drain.

3　Braise the onion in the red wine with the garlic, Thai red curry paste, coconut, lime juice, cilantro, parsley, salt and ground Thai green peppercorns.

4　Add the tomatoes and cook for 1 hour, stirring frequently, until the sauce becomes thick.

5　Pre-heat the oven to gas mark 3, 325°F.

6　Brush a 7 sq in baking tray with oil and ladle in 3 tablespoons of sauce. Cover with a layer of softened lasagne, add another layer of sauce and then a layer of zucchini. Repeat this layering three times, finishing with zucchini on top.

7　Cover the pan and bake for 20 minutes.

8　Garnish with Parmesan shavings and spoonfuls of Asian pesto.

BEETROOT DIM SUM WITH ASIAN PESTO

SEE PAGE 54

INGREDIENTS

1 large beetroot, 4 tbsps Asian pesto (for recipe see page 61). **For the dim sum:** 2 cups rice flour, 1 cup hot water, 1 tbsp chopped fresh cilantro, pinch of saffron, salt and pepper.

METHOD

1 Cook the beetroot in slightly salted water until tender. Drain, cool, peel and slice thinly into julienne. Set aside.

2 Mix the rice flour and hot water together slowly to make a dough. Add cilantro and saffron to taste and season with salt and pepper. The dough should be firm but soft. Let it rest for 30 minutes.

3 Roll the dough out thinly and cut into 15 x 3" diameter circles.

4 Fill each dim sum circle with cooked beetroot, reserving some for the garnish. Close the pasta by folding each circle in half, then pinching the edges together.

5 Steam the dim sum over rapidly boiling water for 3-4 minutes.

6 Toss the dim sum in the pesto to coat and garnish with remaining beetroot.

STIR FRIED PASTA WITH CHINESE RED SPINACH AND PHEASANT

SEE PAGE 55

INGREDIENTS

4 pheasant breasts, 1/2 lb shell pasta, 1 cup chicken stock, 1 tsp olive oil, 1 tsp sesame oil, 2 tsps minced garlic, 1 tsp chopped fresh ginger, 1 cup firmly packed red spinach. **For the seasoning:** 1 tsp soya sauce, 1 tsp mild chili sauce, 2 tsps cornstarch, 2 tsps chicken stock.

METHOD

1 Remove the bones and skin from the pheasant and thickly slice the breast. Set aside.

2 Cook the pasta in the chicken stock, drain and keep warm.

3 Heat the olive and sesame oils in a pan and saute the pasta. Add the garlic, ginger and spinach and continue to cook for 3 minutes.

4 Add the soya sauce and chili sauce.

5 Mix the cornstarch with the 2 tsps of chicken stock and add to the pasta mixture to bind.

6 Meanwhile stir fry the pheasant breast slices in a wok for approximately 1 minute, until the flesh is cooked well on the outside and is still red on the inside. Be careful not to overcook.

7 Fold the cooked pheasant into the pasta and serve hot.

CHINESE HAM AND ANISE BASIL WITH FETTUCINE

SEE PAGE 62

INGREDIENTS

1 lb fettucine, 1 tsp minced garlic, 1/2 tbsp chili oil,
1 tbsp butter, 3/4 cup arugula, 1/4 cup shredded
Chinese ham, 1 tsp whole anise basil leaves,
1/4 cup grated Parmesan cheese.
For the tomato concasse: 1/4 lb fresh tomatoes,
3/4 cup tomato juice, 1 tbsp red wine.
For the sauce: 3 tbsps yoghurt (low-fat), 1 tsp minced
fresh anise basil.

METHOD

1   Cook the fettucine in boiling water until it is
    'al dente'.
2   To make the concasse, peel, seed and dice the
    tomatoes and simmer, together with the red wine,
    until soft and thick.
3   Saute the garlic in a mixture of the chili oil and
    butter. Add the pasta, toss and cook for 1 - 2
    minutes. Wash and tear three quarters of the
    arugula and add to the pasta, along with the ham
    and whole anise basil leaves. Continue to cook
    until heated through.
4   Mix the sauce ingredients together and stir into the
    hot pasta.
5   Put the pasta on the plates, top with the tomato
    concasse and garnish with the Parmesan cheese.
    Decorate with the remaining arugula.

ASIAN PESTO

INGREDIENTS

2 1/4 cups citrus olive oil, 2 tsps sesame oil, 3/4 cup fresh
cilantro sprigs, 1/2 cup parsley, 2 oz red spinach leaves,
1/2 cup fresh Vietnamese basil, 1 cup purple basil, 2 tsps
minced garlic, 1 tsp chili flakes, 1/2 cup unsalted
peanuts, salt and pepper.

METHOD

Pour oils into a blender, add the remaining ingredients
(peanuts last) and season. If the consistency is too thick,
add some additional citrus olive oil. This recipe makes
more pesto than you'll need but it keeps well
in the fridge and can be used in other recipes.

CITRUS OIL

INGREDIENTS

4 cups green virgin olive oil, 7 limes, juice of 4 mandarin
oranges, 1/2 cup Mandarin liqueur.

METHOD

1   Cut limes in half and squeeze slightly.
2   Add to the oil, together with the mandarin orange
    juice and Mandarin liqueur.
3   Seal tightly and keep for at least 14 days
    before use.

VEGETARIAN

All recipes serve four people

SWEET AND SOUR WOK-COOKED VEGETABLES WITH TOFU

SEE PAGE 64

INGREDIENTS

For the sweet and sour sauce: 2 1/4 cups plain tomato sauce (see page 69), 2 tsps freshly minced garlic, 1/2 tsp dried basil, 1/2 tsp celery seed, 4 tsps rice wine vinegar, 1/2 cup apple juice concentrate, 1/2 tsp tamari (soya) sauce, 1/4 tsp ground cardamom, 1/2 tsp fresh cilantro sprigs, 1/2 cup water.
For the vegetables: 1 cup fresh shiitake mushrooms, 1/2 cup dry sherry, 1 cup thinly sliced onions, 1/2 cup dry white wine, 1/2 cup sliced chanterelles, 1 cup julienned red bell peppers, 1/4 cup julienned carrots, 1/2 cup broccoli flowerets, 1/2 cup whole snow peas, 1/4 cup shredded Chinese cabbage, 1/4 cup fresh pineapple chunks, 1 cup firm tofu cubes, 1/4 cup mung bean sprouts, 1 tsp toasted sesame seeds.

METHOD

1 Combine the ingredients for the sauce and simmer for 15 minutes.
2 Soak the shiitake mushrooms in the sherry for about 10 minutes. Drain; remove the stems and slice caps thinly. Reserve the sherry to use if more liquid is needed when braising the vegetables.
3 In a wok, braise the onions in white wine for approximately 10 minutes until they are soft.
4 Add the chanterelles and soaked shiitake and cook for 5 minutes over a high heat, stirring frequently.
5 Add the pepper and carrot, cover and cook for 5 minutes.
6 Add the broccoli, snow peas (with their ends snapped off), cabbage, pineapple and tofu. Cover and cook for 2 minutes.
7 Add the sprouts and cook for another 1 - 2 minutes.
8 Toss the vegetables with the sauce and the sesame seeds.
9 Season to taste and serve with rice.

SOBA NOODLES WITH GREEN MUSTARD LEAVES AND TOFU

SEE PAGE 65

INGREDIENTS

1 1/4 lb broccoli flowerets, 2 cups sliced carrots, 1 cup cauliflower flowerets, 12 - 15 large sliced mushrooms, 1 1/2 cups diced fresh tofu, 1 cup green mustard leaves, 9 oz soba (buckwheat) noodles, 1 cup misoyaki sauce*, toasted sesame seeds, 3 tbsps sesame oil.

METHOD

1 Steam all the vegetables, except the green mustard leaves, together with the tofu, over boiling water until 'al dente'.
2 Bring a pan of water to the boil. Plunge the soba noodles into the water for 30 seconds. Drain.
3 Pour the misoyaki sauce over the noodles, add the steamed vegetables and the washed raw green mustard leaves. Mix well and season.
4 Garnish with the sesame seeds and a few drops of sesame oil. Serve with a good chili sauce.

*available from Japanese food stores

BROCCOLI WITH HONEY AND MUSTARD SAUCE

SEE PAGE 66

INGREDIENTS

2 cups broccoli flowerets, 4 oz yellow plum tomatoes, 4 oz cherry tomatoes. For the sauce: 7 tbsps chicken stock, 2 tbsps freshly chopped herbs (basil, chervil, lemon leaves), 3 tbsps Dijon mustard, 7 tbsps honey, 1/4 tsp freshly ground black pepper.

METHOD

1 Blanch or steam the broccoli and tomatoes.
2 Mix together the sauce ingredients and bring to a boil.
3 Pour over vegetables.

CAMPHOR-SMOKED ASPARAGUS WITH ROASTED RED PEPPERS

SEE PAGE 67

INGREDIENTS

1 lb fresh asparagus, 1 red bell pepper, 7 oz baby artichokes. **For the dressing:** 1 tsp freshly minced garlic, 1/2 cup balsamic vinegar, 4 drops sesame oil, 1 tsp Asian pesto (recipe on page 61), salt. **For the garnish:** 2 lemons, quartered.

SPECIAL EQUIPMENT

1 smoker or wok, 1 lb camphor wood chips

METHOD

1   Remove the tough lowest inches of the asparagus stems.
2   Place wood chips into either a professional smoker or the bottom of a wok. If the latter, place a metal grid over the chips, on top of which position some aluminium foil.
3   Heat to approximately 400°F and when the chips are smoking place the asparagus into the smoker or on to the aluminium foil. Smoke for approximately 5 minutes, taking care not to let the smoke become too over-powering.
4   Roast the red pepper in a very hot oven for 20 - 30 minutes, turning occasionally to ensure even cooking. Remove when the skin has darkened and blistered.
5   Transfer the pepper to a bowl, cover with aluminium foil and leave to cool. After 30 minutes, peel off the skin, remove the seeds and slice.
6   Remove all the leaves from the artichokes, cut in half, remove the hairy chokes and brush with lemon juice. Boil in vegetable stock until cooked.
7   Combine the dressing ingredients and marinate the asparagus in 1/3, the peppers in 1/3 and the artichokes in the remaining 1/3.
8   Put the red pepper on the plates, top with the asparagus and decorate with the artichokes. Garnish with the lemon quarters.

WOK-FRIED CANTONESE VEGETABLES WITH WHITE RADISH

SEE PAGE 70

INGREDIENTS

1 1/2 oz Chinese glass noodles, 1/2 cup firmly packed spinach, 1/4 cup sliced carrots, 1 cup bean sprouts, 1/2 cup sliced Chinese cabbage, 1/2 cup quartered bamboo shoots, 1 cup bak choi, 1 cup sliced Asian mushrooms, 1 cup cauliflower flowerets, 1 cup shredded white radish, 1 tsp sesame oil, 1 tsp minced garlic, 2 cups vegetable stock, **For the marinade:** 1 tsp soya sauce, 1 tsp wine vinegar, 1 tsp cornstarch, 1/4 tsp ginger, 1/4 tsp fresh cilantro sprigs, 1/4 tsp chili sauce.

METHOD

1   Boil the glass noodles for about 4 minutes in salt water. Drain and chill.
2   Combine all the marinade ingredients.
3   Blanch the spinach, carrots, bean sprouts, Chinese cabbage, bamboo shoots, bak choi, Asian mushrooms, cauliflower and shredded white radish. Remove and marinate for 30 minutes.
4   Heat the sesame oil and stir fry the garlic until golden.
5   Drain the vegetables and add to the sizzling garlic.
6   Add the noodles and when heated through season to taste.
7   Add the vegetable stock and heat through.
8   Place the noodles and vegetables in individual dishes and serve hot.

TOMATO SAUCE

INGREDIENTS

2 lbs ripe tomatoes, 1 onion, 1 clove garlic, 2 tsps olive oil, 1 tbsp tomato paste, 1 tbsp shredded basil, 1 sprig rosemary, 4 cups chicken stock, 2 cups tomato juice.

METHOD

1   Wash, de-seed and dice tomatoes.
2   Dice onion, crush garlic and saute together with olive oil.
3   Add tomatoes and braise for 10 minutes. Add the tomato paste and herbs. Pour in the stock and tomato juice and simmer over a low heat for 50 minutes until thick. Strain.

SEAFOOD

All recipes serve four people

ROASTED MONK FISH WITH BASIL AND CURRY SAUCE

INGREDIENTS

4 x 5 oz fillets of monk fish, 3 tbsps light soya sauce. **For the rice:** 1/2 lb basmati rice, 2 1/4 cups water, 1 tbsp butter, 1/4 tsp salt, 3 tbsps coconut milk, 2 tsps shredded basil. **For the curry sauce:** 1 tbsp clarified butter, 2 cloves minced garlic, 3 tbsps spicy curry powder, 1 tsp cumin, 4 cups chicken stock, 1 peeled, cored and diced apple, 2 diced plum tomatoes. Garnish: 1/2 lb sliced yellow zucchini, 1/2 cup bean sprouts, basil leaves. **To serve:** steamed rice.

METHOD

1   Brush the monk fish fillets with the soya sauce and pan fry until golden brown. Keep warm.

2   Add the basmati rice to the water, add the salt and bring to the boil. Lower the heat, cover and cook for approximately 15 minutes. Add the coconut milk and simmer for 3 minutes until absorbed. Mix in the shredded basil.

3   Heat the clarified butter and saute the garlic. Add the curry powder, cumin and 4 tbsps of stock to make a thick paste. Cook for 3 - 4 minutes, add the remaining stock and reduce by half. Add the apple and tomatoes. Cook for a further 5 minutes and strain.

4   Saute the zucchini until soft and steam the bean sprouts with salt and pepper.

5   Spoon a bed of rice on to each plate, top with the monk fish, zucchini, bean sprouts, basil leaves and serve with the sauce.

VIETNAMESE CRAB CAKES WITH CHILI AND MUSTARD

INGREDIENTS

8 crab claws. **For the crab cakes:** 1/4 lb crab meat, preferably from Vietnam, 1 cup mashed potatoes, 1 tbsp diced yellow bell pepper, 1 tbsp diced red bell pepper, 1 tbsp chopped shallots, 1 tbsp minced garlic, 1/2 cup chopped tomatoes, 1 tsp chopped fresh Vietnamese basil, salt and pepper. **For frying:** 2 egg whites, 3 tbsps fine, dry white breadcrumbs, 4 tbsps olive oil. **For the sauce:** 1 cup chicken stock, 1 cup crab jus (see below), 1 tsp prepared mustard, 2 tsps chili sauce, 2 tsps oyster sauce, salt and pepper. **Garnish:** mixed lettuce salad and steamed fresh zucchini, 1 tsp chopped fresh mint, chili sauce.

METHOD

1   Steam the crab claws for 4 minutes. Carefully remove the meat from the shells to use as garnish. The shells should be kept for making the crab jus.
2   Combine all ingredients for the crab cakes, season with salt and pepper and form into eight patties.
3   Dip the patties in the egg white and then in the breadcrumbs. Pan fry slowly until golden brown.
4   Combine all the sauce ingredients, adjust seasoning and bring to a boil. Keep warm.
5   Place two patties on each plate and garnish with the freshly cooked crab claw meat. Pour sauce around patties, add salad leaves and zucchini and sprinkle with the chopped mint. Serve with chili sauce.

CRAB JUS

INGREDIENTS

1/2 lb crab shells, 2 tbsps diced tomatoes, 1 sliced carrot, 1/2 sliced onion, 1 tsp minced garlic, 1 tsp tomato paste, 1 cup white wine, 1 cup chicken stock, 1 bay leaf, 1 tsp fresh cilantro leaves.

METHOD

Roast the shells in a small amount of olive oil until well coated. Add the vegetables and continue to saute until they soften. Add the tomato paste, stir and cook for another 3 - 4 minutes. Deglaze with the wine. Add the stock, bay leaf and fresh cilantro leaves. Simmer for 30 minutes. Strain. Return to heat and simmer, uncovered, until reduced by half.

CARDAMOM-STEAMED SALMON ON LONG BEAN SALAD

INGREDIENTS

1/2 lb salmon fillet, 1 sliced zucchini, 1 tbsp butter, 1/2 lb long beans. **For the fish seasoning:** 3 tbsps lemon juice, 6 tbsps olive oil, 1 1/2 tsps ground cardamom, 1 tsp ground star anise, 1/2 tsp freshly ground black pepper.
For the salad: 1/2 lb salad hearts, 3 tbsps shredded Thai basil, 1 tbsp lemon balm. **Garnish:** 1 tsp Thai basil.

METHOD

1   Skin the salmon and chop into cubes. Combine fish seasoning ingredients and mix half of this mixture with the salmon. Reserve other half for the salad.
2   Saute the zucchini in the butter for 2 - 3 minutes, add the fish, cover and steam over a low heat for 2 minutes. Make sure the fish is not overcooked.
3   Cut the long beans into 3" sections and steam in a separate pan.
4   When still hot, mix the salad hearts with the long beans, the Thai basil and the lemon balm.
5   Top with the salmon, pour over remaining marinade and decorate with the Thai basil.

SOLE FILLET WITH FIRE-ROASTED MUSHROOMS AND LIME TURMERIC SAUCE

SEE PAGE 76

INGREDIENTS

4 skinless sole fillets, 1 tbsp melted butter.
For the mushrooms: 1 tsp minced onion, 1 tsp minced garlic, 1 1/2 tsps olive oil, 1/2 lb mixed sliced mushrooms (chanterelles, stone mushrooms, button mushrooms), 1 tbsp white wine vinegar, 2 tsps chopped fresh basil, 1 tsp thyme, 1 tsp rosemary, salt and pepper, 1 cup mung bean vermicelli.
For lime-turmeric sauce: 2 cups chicken stock, 1/2 tsp turmeric, 1 lime, quartered, 2 tsps tomato paste, 1/2 tsp minced ginger, 1 sliced green onion.
Garnish: fresh cilantro leaves and chili flakes, shredded green onion, 16 steamed snow peas.

METHOD

1   Brush the sole fillets with melted butter, then either steam for 10 minutes, or pan fry, until cooked.
2   Saute the onion and garlic in the olive oil, until golden. Add the mushrooms and continue to cook for 1 - 2 minutes. Deglaze with the vinegar and season with the basil, thyme, rosemary, salt and pepper.
3   Blanch the vermicelli. Mix with the mushrooms.
4   Combine all the ingredients for the sauce and simmer until the flavors are blended - approximately 15 minutes. Remove the lime.
    Puree the rest in a blender to desired texture - either smooth or coarsely ground. Season to taste.
5   Place the mushrooms and vermicelli on the plates. Top with the sole fillets and sprinkle with the cilantro leaves, chili flakes and green onion.
6   Top with the snow peas and serve sauce separately.

BABY TURBOT WITH GARLIC, BASIL AND A RED BEAN SAUCE

SEE PAGE 77

INGREDIENTS

4 - 5 oz baby turbot fillets, 1 tsp melted butter, salt, 2 tbsps curry powder, 1/2 tsp anise, 1 sprig rosemary, 2 tsps minced garlic, 2 tbsps shredded basil.
For the vegetables: 2 sliced raw shallots, 4 oz cooked rice noodles, 2 julienned raw carrots, 1 tsp shredded cilantro leaves, 2 tsps lemon juice.
For the red bean sauce: 1/2 cup cooked red beans, 1 cup chicken stock, 3 tbsps mild chili sauce, 2 tbsps diced onion, 2 tsps minced garlic.
Garnish: marjoram leaves.

METHOD

1   Mix the salt, curry powder, anise, rosemary, minced garlic and basil together.
2   Brush the turbot fillets with the melted butter and then smear with the spice mix.
3   Cook the fish for 8 minutes at gas mark 9, 475°F in the oven.
4   Mix together the shallots, noodles, carrots, cilantro and lemon juice.
5   Blend the beans with the chicken stock, add the chili sauce, onions and garlic.
6   Place the raw vegetables and noodles on the plates and top with the hot fish. Serve the sauce on the side.

SESAME-CRUSTED SCALLOPS ON RED CHINESE SPINACH LEAVES

SEE PAGE 78

INGREDIENTS

28 medium sized scallops, 1 egg white, 1 tsp lemon juice, 2 tsps toasted sesame seeds, salt.
For the sauce: 1 cup chicken stock, 1 tsp balsamic vinegar, 2 sliced shallots, 1 tsp crushed garlic, 1/2 lemon, 1/4 cup diced tomato, 1 tsp shredded cilantro leaves, 2 tsps cornstarch, 1 tsp wasabi.
For the salad: 1/2 lb red Chinese spinach leaves, 2 endive, 1/4 cup diced tofu, 1 tsp chopped parsley.
Garnish: lobster claws, chili flakes.

METHOD

1   Coat raw scallops with a mixture of the egg white and lemon juice. Coat with sesame seeds, season and pan fry in olive or corn oil until golden brown. Keep warm.
2   Combine all the sauce ingredients, except for the cornstarch and the wasabi. Simmer gently and briefly until all flavors have blended. Thicken with cornstarch mixed to a paste with a little water. Stir in the wasabi.
3   Mix the spinach with endive leaves, tofu, parsley and cooked lobster claw. Season with the sauce. Place on the plates, top with the sesame-crusted scallops and garnish with chili flakes.

SOYA-STEAMED LOBSTER WITH SNAKE BEANS

SEE PAGE 79

INGREDIENTS

2 whole lobsters, 4 cups vegetable stock.
For the filling: 1 tbsp soya sauce, 2 tsps minced garlic, 2 tsps minced ginger, 1 tsp chopped shallots, 1/2 lb chopped tomatoes, 2 tsps basil, 1 tsp cilantro leaves, 1/2 tsp lemon juice. For the vegetables: 1 cup snake beans, 1 cup straw mushrooms.
Garnish: 2 lemons, halved, 1/2 cup grated Parmesan cheese, 1 cup deep fried vermicelli.

METHOD

1   Bring the vegetable stock to a boil. Add the lobsters and simmer for 10 minutes until nearly cooked. Drain and cool.
2   Remove the claws, crack and extract the meat. Cut each lobster in half and remove the meat from the shells. Marinate the lobster meat in the soya sauce, 1 tsp minced garlic and 1 tsp ginger and replace meat in half lobster shells. Do not overcook.
3   Saute the remaining garlic and ginger, together with the chopped shallot in olive or corn oil until soft. Add tomatoes, basil, cilantro and lemon juice and top the ready steamed lobsters.
4   Serve with steamed snake beans and straw mushrooms. Garnish with half a lemon, grated Parmesan cheese and deep fried vermicelli.

STEAMED GAROUPA WITH LIME AND GREEN ONION

SEE PAGE 80

INGREDIENTS

1 x 1 1/2 lb fresh garoupa, juice of 2 kaffir limes,
1 cup broccoli flowerets, 1 cup shredded cabbage,
For the sauce: 2 cups chicken stock, 1 cup soya sauce,
salt and pepper. **Garnish:** 2 tsps cilantro leaves, 1/4 cup
diced tomato, 2 shredded green onions.

METHOD

1   Clean and gut the fish. Season with the lime juice.
2   Place in a steamer and cook for 15 minutes.
3   Steam the vegetables. Keep warm.
4   Mix the chicken stock with the soya sauce, season and
    bring to a boil.
5   Place the garoupa on a large fish platter. Decorate
    with the vegetables. Pour the sauce over the fish
    and vegetables.
6   Garnish with the cilantro, tomato and green onions.

CHOI SUM WITH SWEET POTATOES AND AN EGG WHITE ABALONE CRUST

SEE PAGE 81

INGREDIENTS

2 - 3 cooked sweet potatoes, 1 tsp butter, 1 small sliced
onion, 1 sliced leek, 1/2 cup mixed sliced mushrooms,
1 tsp minced garlic, 1 tbsp fresh chopped ginger,
1/2 lb choi sum, 5 diced tomatoes, 1 chopped green
onion, 1/2 tsp crushed green peppercorns, 3 egg whites,
1/4 cup finely chopped abalone.

METHOD

1   Peel the cooked potatoes, cut in small strips and
    saute in the butter.
2   Pan fry the onion and leek. Add the mushrooms
    and cook.
3   Preheat oven to gas mark 6, 400°F.
4   In another pan saute the garlic and ginger and when
    softened, add the choi sum.
5   Combine the choi sum mixture with the onion,
    leek and mushroom mixture. Stir in the tomato
    and green onion and season with salt and pepper.
    Put into oven-proof dishes.
6   Whisk the egg whites until stiff, add the chopped
    abalone and season. Pour onto the top of the
    vegetable mixture and bake for 2 minutes in the
    oven until brown.

CRISPY SALMON WITH SAFFRON PEPPER JUS AND MIZUNA GREENS

SEE PAGE 88

INGREDIENTS

4 x 5 oz salmon fillets with skin, 1/2 tsp soya sauce, 1/2 tsp red wine vinegar, salt and pepper, 2 potatoes, 2 cups warm low fat milk, 2 tbsps butter, 1 tbsp truffle jus (optional), salt and pepper. **For the salad:** 3/4 lb mizuna greens, 1 tsp shredded basil, 2 sliced shallots, 2 tbsps soya sauce, 1 tbsp sesame oil, juice of 1/2 lemon. **For the sauce:** 1/2 cup sliced shiitake mushrooms, 1 cup chicken stock, pinch saffron threads, 8 tbsps virgin olive oil, 4 tbsps balsamic vinegar, 2 tsps diced tomato, 1/2 tsp coarsely crushed black peppercorns.

METHOD

1 Combine the soya sauce and vinegar. Brush the salmon fillets with this and broil, on the skin side only, for 6 minutes at a high heat.

2 Boil the potatoes, cool and peel.

3 Grate finely into a saucepan and slowly add the warm milk, stirring to make the mixture smooth. Warm gently and add the butter. When it has melted, season with truffle jus, salt and pepper.

4 For the salad, combine the soya sauce, sesame oil and lemon juice. Pour over the greens, basil and shallots and toss gently.

5 Quickly saute the sliced mushrooms.

6 Warm the chicken stock. Infuse the saffron threads in the stock for about 10 minutes. Combine with the olive oil, balsamic vinegar, tomato, black peppercorns and mushrooms. Season to taste.

7 Place the mashed potatoes in the middle of the plate, arrange the salmon on top, spoon the sauce around and dress with the salad.

MEAT AND POULTRY

All recipes serve four people

TEPPANYAKI VEGETABLES WITH PIGEON AND ASIAN PESTO

INGREDIENTS

2 pigeons, 4 tbsps Asian pesto (see recipe on page 61). **For the pigeon marinade:** 2 tsps soya sauce, 1 tsp sesame oil, 1/2 tbsp crushed cilantro seeds, 2 tsps minced garlic. **For the vegetables:** 100g diced tofu, 1/4 lb asparagus, 1/4 cup carrot sticks, 1/4 cup snow peas, 1/4 cup sliced red bell pepper, 1 tbsp olive oil. **Garnish:** 3/4 lb rice noodles.

METHOD

1   Marinate pigeons for 10 minutes in soya sauce, sesame oil, crushed cilantro seeds and minced garlic.
2   Sear over a medium heat for 1-2 minutes until skin is crispy.
3   Place pigeons into pre-heated oven at 200°C and roast for 8 minutes until medium (pink). De-bone pigeon breasts and keep warm.
4   Saute diced tofu in a little oil until golden brown. Keep warm.
5   Put the remaining vegetables in a pan and roast with the olive oil and Asian pesto at gas mark 7, 425°F until well done.
6   Deep fry rice noodles until very crispy.
7   Place the teppanyaki vegetables on the plates and arrange pigeon breasts on top. Garnish with deep fried noodles.

CILANTRO-ENCRUSTED BEEF WITH MUSHROOMS AND WOK-FRIED BELL PEPPERS

INGREDIENTS

4 organically-fed beef tenderloin (5 oz each), 1/2 tsp crushed cilantro seeds, 2 tsps crushed black pepper.
For the mushrooms: 1 tsp crushed garlic, 1 small chopped onion, 1 tsp butter, 2 tsps sesame oil,
3/4 lb assorted sliced mushrooms (shiitake, enoki, stone mushrooms, button mushrooms), 2 tsps chopped fresh basil.
For the potato: 1 large potato. **For the side vegetables:** 1 green bell pepper, 1 yellow bell pepper,
1 red bell pepper, 1 lb green asparagus.

METHOD

1   Season the beef tenderloin with crushed cilantro and black pepper and roast at gas mark 4, 350°F for approximately 6 - 7 minutes until cooked medium rare.
2   Saute the garlic and onion in the butter until softened.
3   Add the mushrooms and basil and continue to cook until the mushrooms are done.
4   Cut the potato into 1" x 4" sticks and blanch. Fry in vegetable oil until crisp, keep warm.
5   Cut the peppers in half, remove the seeds and slice. Peel the asparagus. Wok fry both the peppers and asparagus. Season with salt and pepper.
6   Place two potato sticks on each plate. Top with the tenderloin, followed by the peppers and asparagus and then the mushrooms. Serve with a light beef jus.

BEEF JUS
INGREDIENTS

1 cup sliced shallots, 2 tsps crushed garlic, 2 tsps shredded cilantro, 3 tbsps red wine vinegar, 2 cups red wine,
1 cup diced tomato, 4 cups beef stock, 1 - 2 tsps cornstarch, salt and pepper.

Saute the shallots and garlic and when softened add the cilantro sprigs. Deglaze the pan with the red wine vinegar, add the red wine and the diced tomatoes and cook over a slow heat until the liquid has reduced by half. Add the beef stock and cook over a slow heat until again it has reduced by half. Strain the mixture. Mix the cornstarch with 4 tsps of water and bind the jus. Season to taste.

BABY LAMB MARINATED WITH SESAME OIL, RED CURRY AND MINT

INGREDIENTS

1/2 lb baby lamb fillet, 1 tbsp sesame oil, 1/2 tbsp red curry paste, 1 cup lamb sauce (recipe below), 2 - 3 endive,
1 - 2 crushed cloves of garlic, 1 tsp lemon thyme, 1 tsp chopped cilantro leaves, salt and pepper.
Garnish: 1 endive, 10 halved cherry tomatoes.

METHOD

1   Slice the lamb, marinate with a mixture of the sesame oil and red curry paste.
2   Saute the lamb for a few minutes until meat is rare. Deglaze the pan with lamb sauce.
3   Cut the endive in half.
4   Add the endive, garlic, lemon thyme and cilantro to the pan, reduce heat and braise - keeping the meat medium rare.
    Season with salt and pepper.
5   Arrange the raw endive around the edges of a platter, put the lamb in the middle of the plate and garnish with the cherry
    tomato halves and lemon thyme.

LAMB SAUCE

INGREDIENTS

1/2 lb lamb bones, 2 tbsps olive oil, 1/4 cup diced tomato, 1/4 cup sliced celery, 1 diced onion, 2 tsps minced garlic,
1 tsp basil, 1 tsp tarragon, 1 tsp mint, 4 cups water, salt and pepper, 1 cup red wine (optional).

METHOD

1   Clean and cut the bones. Pre-heat oven to gas mark 6, 400°F and roast the bones in olive oil until dark brown.
2   Scoop off any liquid fat. Add the vegetables and herbs to the pan and cook until they are soft.
3   Remove vegetables and bones, put into saucepan and add the water. Bring to the boil and then reduce heat and
    simmer for 2 hours. During simmering skim the surface of the sauce to remove frothy matter.
4   Strain and reduce by half. Season.
5   If using red wine, add to the pan and reduce again by half.

CAYENNE PEPPER GLAZED PIGEON WITH BAMBOO SHOOTS

SEE PAGE 94

INGREDIENTS

2 pigeons.

For the cayenne pepper glaze: 1 cup barbecue sauce, 1 cup tomato ketchup, 2 tsps soya sauce, dash cayenne pepper, 2 tsps minced garlic, juice of 1 lemon, 1 tsp red wine vinegar. For the vegetables: 2 tsps sesame oil, 1 cup quartered bamboo shoots, 1/4 cup dry fungus, 1/2 lb bean sprouts, 1/2 cup snow peas, 1 cup thinly sliced carrot, 1/2 cup blanched bean thread noodles (mung bean vermicelli), 1 tsp sesame oil.
Garnish: 1/2 tsp toasted sesame seeds.

METHOD

1   Soak the dry fungus for 10 hours.
2   Cut each pigeon in half and sear quickly.
3   Combine all the ingredients for the cayenne pepper glaze and brush over the pigeon. Roast at gas mark 6, 400°F for 6 minutes. Divide the breast from the leg, and if necessary place the leg back in the oven as it should be well done.
4   In a hot pan, stir fry all the vegetables and noodles in sesame oil and season to taste.
5   Garnish with the sesame seeds.

ORIENTAL SPICED VEAL CUTLET

SEE PAGE 95

INGREDIENTS

4 veal cutlets (5 oz each), 4 tbsps Oriental spice powder (recipe below), 2 tsps olive oil.
For the vegetables: 1 cup sliced cabbage, 1/2 cup snow peas, 1 cup bak choi. For the sauce: 1 cup balsamic vinegar, 1 cup vegetable stock, 1 tsp chopped parsley, 1/2 tsp minced garlic, 1 tsp soya sauce, salt and pepper, 1/2 tsp cornstarch. To serve: steamed rice.

METHOD

1   Season the cutlets with the spice powder; coat lightly with olive oil and roast at gas mark 9, 475°F for 10 minutes.
2   In the remaining olive oil saute the cabbage, snow peas and bak choi. Keep warm.
3. Remove the meat from the roast pan, heat the dripping and deglaze with the balsamic vinegar.
4   Add the stock, parsley and garlic. Bring to the boil and simmer briefly. Adjust seasoning with soya sauce and/or salt and pepper. Thicken with cornstarch mixed to a paste with some water.
5   Place the veal cutlets on the plates and serve with rice and vegetables. Pour a little sauce over the rice and the meat.

ORIENTAL SPICE POWDER

Mix together 5 tsps 5-spice powder, 1 tsp crushed cilantro seeds, 1 1/2 tsp mild yellow curry powder and 1/2 tsp crushed black pepper.

MONGOLIAN LAMB SHANK WITH GINGER-FLAVORED VEGETABLES

SEE PAGE 96

INGREDIENTS

4 small lamb shanks, with the bone (no more than 1/2 lb each). **For the vegetables:** 1 tsp sesame oil, 1 cup diced cucumber, 1 cup diced carrots, 1/2 cup diced tomato. **For the braising sauce:** 1 cup red wine, 2 1/2 cups chicken stock, 2 tsps tomato paste, 1/2 cup finely diced onion, 1 tsp chopped garlic, 2 bay leaves, 3 tsps chopped ginger, 1 tsp chopped red chilies. **For serving:** 1/2 lb taro, 1/2 lb potato, 1 cup skimmed milk, 2 tbsps butter, 1 tsp dry mint, salt and pepper. **Garnish:** 1/2 cup whole green onions, 1/2 cup snow peas.

METHOD

1   Sear the shanks quickly in a hot pan to give them color.
2   Mix the vegetables with the sesame oil and place in a square roasting pan. Arrange the lamb shanks on top. Pour on the red wine and chicken stock and add the tomato paste, onion, garlic, bay leaves, ginger and red chilies. Cover. Braise for 1 hour at gas mark 6, 400°F.
3   Remove vegetables from roasting pan to avoid overcooking and keep warm. Return lamb shanks to oven for a further hour, frequently basting with the juices.
4   Boil taro and potatoes separately and when cooked remove the skins and push through a potato grater. Mix together in a hot pan with warmed skimmed milk and butter. Season with dry mint and salt and pepper.
5   Steam the snow peas and spring onions.
6   Place the mixed taro and potato mash on the plates, top with the lamb shanks and serve with diced vegetable mixture and green onions and snow peas. Serve the sauce in which the meat and vegetables were cooked as gravy.

ROSE LIQUEUR GLAZED DUCK BREAST WITH A BOUQUET OF GREENS

SEE PAGE 97

INGREDIENTS

2 duck breasts (preferably from free-range ducks, each 1/2 lb, with skin). **For the marinade:** 1 tsp soya sauce, 1 tsp rose liqueur*, 1 tsp salt, 1 tsp ground ginger, 1/2 tsp ground cinnamon, 1/2 tsp ground black pepper. **Vegetables:** 1/2 lb carrots, 1/2 lb white radish, 1/2 lb snow peas. **For the salad:** 3/4 lb mixed salad hearts. **For the salad dressing:** 2 tsps shredded basil, 2 chopped shallots, 1 tsp chopped ginger, 8 tbsps olive oil, 4 tbsps red wine vinegar.

METHOD

1   Trim as much fat as possible off the duck breasts, leaving just a thin layer between the skin and flesh.
2   Mix the marinade ingredients together and rub well into the duck skin.
3   Roast at gas mark 3, 325°F for approximately 7 minutes. Remove and keep warm.
4   Trim the carrots and white radish to 1 1/2" sticks and boil for 8 minutes, then roast in the duck juices together with the snow peas for a further 15 minutes.
5   Combine the dressing ingredients and toss with the salad hearts.
6   Slice the breasts and arrange on the plates. Add a side serving of tossed salad plus the roasted carrots, white radish and snow peas.

*available from Chinese dry goods stores.

SILK CHICKEN CURRY WITH NAAN BREAD

SEE PAGE 98

INGREDIENTS

For the curry: 2 tsps butter, 1 1/2 lb diced skinless silk chicken, 3 tsps Sri Lankan curry powder, 4 cups chicken stock, 1 stalk of lemon grass, 1/2 cup finely chopped onion, 2 bay leaves, 2 tsps tomato paste, 1 tsp minced garlic, 2 tsps cornstarch. Garnish: 8 green onions.

METHOD

1   Heat the butter in a saucepan and add the chicken, then the curry powder.
2   When fragrant, add the stock and the remaining ingredients, except the cornstarch. Simmer for 45 minutes.
3   Mix the cornstarch to a paste with some water and stir in to bind.
4   Remove lemon grass stalk. Garnish with green onions and serve with steamed rice and seasonal vegetables.

NAAN BREAD

INGREDIENTS

3/4 lb flour, 2 1/4 cups water, 1 tsp baking powder, 2 tsps olive oil, 1 egg, 1 tsp sugar, 1 tsp salt.

METHOD

1   Combine all the ingredients, using enough water to make a stiff dough.
2   Make small (3 oz) dough balls. Flatten to make very thin 9" rounds.
3   Pre-heat oven to gas mark 9, 475°F and bake for 2 -3 minutes. (For best results cook in a tandoor or pizza oven).

CONTEMPORARY KIM CHEE WITH HONEY-SMOKED CHICKEN BREAST

SEE PAGE 99

INGREDIENTS

4 chicken breasts, 1 cup chicken stock.
For the chicken marinade: 2 tsps minced garlic, 4 tsps honey, 4 tsps soya sauce.
For the kim chee: 3/4 lb shredded white cabbage, 2 oz white radish (large Oriental type), 1 cup white wine vinegar, 1 cup chili sauce (preferably mild-Korean style), 1 cup chicken stock, 2 lemons (quartered), 4 tsps soya sauce. For the vegetables: 1/2 cup mung bean sprouts, 1 cup firmly packed spinach, 1/2 tsp sesame oil.

METHOD

1   Sear the chicken breasts quickly over a high heat.
2   Mix the chicken marinade together and marinate the breasts for 30 minutes. Smoke the breasts as per the recipe on page 69 for 10 minutes until well done. Keep warm.
2   Marinate the cabbage and diced white radish in a mixture of the vinegar and chili sauce and leave for 1 hour.
3   Put the chicken stock into a pan with the cabbage and the marinade, quartered lemons and soya sauce and cook over a low heat until the cabbage is cooked, yet still a bit crunchy.
4   Saute the mung bean sprouts. At the same time saute the spinach in the sesame oil over high heat.
5   Arrange a portion of pickled cabbage on each plate, top with sliced chicken breasts and serve with the sauteed vegetables.

CHICKEN BREAST WITH BAK CHOI AND BAKED POTATOES

INGREDIENTS

For the chicken: 2 cups chicken stock, 1 sprig rosemary, 4 chicken breasts (1 lb), 4 heads bak choi.

For the sauce: 1 tsp mustard, 1/4 tsp salt, pepper to taste, 4 tsps olive oil, 3 tsps herbed vinegar, 2 tsps chopped tomatoes, 1 tsp minced garlic, 1/2 tsp basil.

For the potato shells: 2 tsps butter, 4 - 6 potatoes, 1 tsp salt.

METHOD

1 Bring the chicken stock, with a sprig of rosemary, to the boil. Add the chicken breasts, reduce the heat to a simmer and slowly cook the chicken for 10 - 12 minutes. Remove and keep warm.

2 Add the bak choi to the simmering stock and cook for 3 minutes. Keep warm.

3 Combine the sauce ingredients and gently heat.

4 Brush a baking tray with the butter and pre-heat it to gas mark 9, 475°F oven.

5 Cut the potatoes (unpeeled) in 1/2" slices. Place on the pre-heated tray, season and bake for 30 minutes.

6 Place a piece of bak choi on each breast, brush with sauce and serve with a few slices of potato.

MEDLEY OF ASIAN VEGETABLES WITH KOBE BEEF

SEE PAGE 106

INGREDIENTS

4 oz baby eggplant, 4 oz shiitake mushrooms, 4 oz green celery, 4 oz okra, 1 red onion, 3 oz lily bulb, 2 shallots, 3 oz yellow and red plum tomatoes, 2 tbsps olive oil, 2 tsps minced garlic, 4 tsps Asian pesto (see recipe on page 61). For the soya hollandaise: 3 egg yolks, 1 tsp balsamic vinegar, 1 tsp minced shallot, 1 tsp soya sauce, 1/2 lb melted butter (preferably clarified), salt and pepper. For topping: 4 oz cold roast Kobe beef sirloin, 2 tsps shredded cilantro leaves, 2 green onions.

METHOD

1 Slice all the vegetables and boil until nearly cooked.

2 Heat the oil, fry the garlic and slowly braise vegetables for 5 minutes. Mix with the Asian pesto.

3 Beat the egg yolks with the balsamic vinegar, shallots and soya sauce in a bowl over hot water, or in a double boiler, until thick and fluffy. Mix with the liquid butter until the consistency is smooth. Season with salt and pepper.

4. Pile the vegetables onto a platter, top with the soya hollandaise and garnish with thick slices of Kobe beef, shredded cilantro leaves amd chopped green onion.

DESSERTS

All recipes serve four people

CINNAMON CHOCOLATE SANDWICHES

INGREDIENTS

For the white chocolate triangles: 4 oz good white chocolate. For the meringue: 4 oz sugar, 1 cup water, 4 egg whites, 3 tsps cinnamon powder, juice of 1 lemon. For the sandwich filling: 1/2 cup raspberries, 1/2 cup blueberries, 1/2 cup strawberries. Garnish: icing sugar, 3 oz good dark chocolate, 8 tbsps fruit puree.

METHOD

1   Melt white chocolate and pour onto a sheet of baking paper. Flatten with a spatula and cool in the fridge until firm. Cut along a ruler into 6 squares with a sharp knife. Cut squares in half to make triangles.
2   Boil the sugar with the water. Cool slightly.
3   Beat the egg whites until frothy and slowly add the sugar water and cinnamon. Lastly, add the lemon juice. Beat the mixture until cool - set aside.
4   Pipe the meringue mixture on top of 4 triangles; place a layer of mixed fruit on top.
5   Top with another chocolate triangle, pipe on more meringue and position another layer of fruit on top.
6   Top with another chocolate triangle. Dust with icing sugar.
7   For decoration only - melt the chocolate and pour on to a flat surface. Allow to cool and cut 8 x 2 1/2" sticks. Make a hole in the top layer with a toothpick and secure chocolate stick in the hole.
8   Serve the chocolate sandwiches with a sauce made from pureed raspberries, mangoes or blueberries.

THAI MELON MEDLEY

3 oz chilled watermelon, 3 oz chilled cantaloupe melon, 3 oz chilled honeydew melon.

Garnish: papaya 'leaf', washed chrysanthemum petals.

METHOD

1   Peel and finely slice all melons.

2   Arrange on plates.

3   Top with papaya 'leaf' and chrysanthemum petals.

GREEN TEA SOUFFLE WITH CRYSTALLIZED ORANGES

SEE PAGE 110

INGREDIENTS

For the custard base: 1 tbsp butter, 4 cups milk, 1/2 tsp green tea powder, 1 vanilla pod (or essence to taste) 1 tbsp self raising flour, 3 tbsps dark rum, juice and zest of 1/2 lemon, For the souffle: 5 egg whites, 3/4 cup sugar, 1 tsp melted butter. Garnish: vanilla ice cream, crystallized oranges and fresh berries.

METHOD

1 Combine the butter, milk and tea powder in a saucepan and bring to the boil. Add the vanilla pod.

2 Mix the flour to a paste with the rum and the lemon juice. Add to the hot milk. Cook, stirring continuously, until thickened. Season with vanilla essence if using - or remove vanilla pod. Cool the mixture to room temperature.

3 Beat the egg whites to soft peaks. Continue beating while adding the sugar. Beat to stiff peaks.

4 Prepare either 4 small souffle dishes, or one large one, by brushing the bottom and edges with melted butter. Coat lightly with sugar. Pre-heat oven to gas mark 3, 375°F.

5 Fold the beaten egg whites into the custard with a few quick, light strokes.

6 Transfer the mixture to the prepared souffle dishes. Set in a bain marie and cook for 15 - 20 minutes.

7 Dust with icing sugar and serve immediately with ice cream and fruit segments.

CRYSTALLIZED ORANGES

INGREDIENTS

2 oranges, 3/4 cup melted butter, 3/4 cup sugar

METHOD

Peel oranges and divide into segments. Remove skin from segments. Dissolve sugar in the melted butter and add segments. Cook until sugar crystallizes on the fruit. Add a dash of Grand Marnier and serve immediately.

HOT KAFFIR LIME TART WITH GINSENG ICE CREAM

SEE PAGE 111

INGREDIENTS

For the sugar dough base: 1 cup butter, 3/4 cup icing sugar, 1 egg, 1 lb sieved self raising flour, vanilla essence. For the filling: 3/4 cup sugar, 1/4 cup mascarpone cheese, 3 eggs, juice of 3 limes, grated zest from one lime, 1 cup cream, 1/2 tsp cornstarch. Garnish: ginseng ice cream (recipe below), basil leaves, orange and lemon zest.

METHOD

1 Cream butter and icing sugar, add the egg and continue to beat until a pale color.

2 Whilst still beating, add the flour and beat minimally. Add the vanilla essence to taste.

3 Gather the dough into a ball, cover with plastic wrap and place in the fridge until firm.

4 Roll out thinly and cut to line a 9"cake tin, 1 1/2" deep. Bake blind for 5 minutes at gas mark 6, 400°F.

5 Mix the sugar with the mascarpone, add the eggs and beat until smooth. Add the lime juice, zest and cream. Finally add the cornstarch.

6 Pour the filling into the half-baked shell. Bake at gas mark 3, 325°F for 25 - 30 minutes.

7 Thinly pare the zest from an orange (preferably a blood orange) and a lemon. Cook in sugared water.

8 Serve the tart with ginseng ice cream topped with the citrus zest and basil leaves.

GINSENG ICE CREAM

INGREDIENTS

4 cups skimmed milk, 3/4 cup caster sugar, 1 vanilla pod, 6 eggs, 3 tbsps ginseng liqueur.

METHOD

1 Bring the milk, sugar and vanilla to a boil.

2 Beat eggs and whisk into the hot milk mixture.

3 Continue to beat until thoroughly blended.

4 As soon as the mixture starts to thicken, remove from the heat and transfer to an ice cream maker.

5 Add ginseng liqueur and follow ice cream maker's instructions.

6 When the ice cream is thick and creamy, remove and freeze until needed.

SWEET GINGERED TEARDROP WITH CHERRIES

SEE PAGE 112

INGREDIENTS

5 oz dark chocolate, 1/4 cup brandy cherries (purchased). For the chocolate cream: 2 oz bitter chocolate, 1/2 cup butter, 2 tbsps cocoa powder. For the sabayon: 3 egg yolks, 1/2 cup sugar, 1 cup white wine, 1 tsp strong coffee powder, 3/4 cup fresh cream, 1/4 cup brandy cherries, 2 tbsps chopped preserved ginger. For the vanilla sauce: 4 cups warm milk, 1/2 vanilla pod, 6 egg yolks, 1 cup sugar. Garnish: brandy cherries, vanilla sauce.

SPECIAL EQUIPMENT

4 plastic strips to form the 'teardrops'

METHOD

1   To make the chocolate cream add the 2 oz bitter chocolate to the butter and cocoa powder and melt over hot water.

2   Whip egg yolks, sugar and white wine over hot water until fluffy - be careful not to scramble eggs. As soon as the mixture triples in size, remove from the heat.

3   Add the melted chocolate and the coffee. When cool fold in the cream, 1/4 cup brandied cherries and the chopped ginger. Add 2 tbsps of the cherry marinade to enhance the chocolate cream. Mix gently.

4   Heat the milk with the 1/2 vanilla pod for several minutes, allowing the vanilla to infuse the milk. Remove pod.

5   Beat the 6 yolks with the sugar. Gradually add the warm milk to the yolks, beating constantly until the mixture has thickened.

6   For the tear as pictured, coat the plastic strips with 5 oz melted chocolate. Allow to cool and form into a teardrop shape.

7   Once set, fill with brandy cherries and chocolate supreme. Place in the fridge to set.

8   Place one tear on each plate and remove plastic strip. Garnish with brandy cherries and a little vanilla sauce.

FIVE SPICE CHOCOLATE MOUSSE

SEE PAGE 113

INGREDIENTS

4 oz dark chocolate, 3/4 oz bitter chocolate, 2 large egg yolks, 2 tsps five spice powder, 4 tbsps brandy, 1 1/2 cups whipped cream, 1 1/2 leaves gelatine, 2 large egg whites, 1/4 cup sugar. For the sauce: 2 tbsps liquid coffee, 4 oz bitter chocolate.

METHOD

1   Melt the chocolates together in a double boiler or over boiling water.

2   Beat the yolks and add to the melted chocolate.

3   Add the five spice powder and brandy, if desired.

4   Whip the cream amd soften the gelatine. Fold both in to the chocolate mixture.

5   Beat the egg whites together with the sugar until stiff.

6   Fold the chocolate mixture into the egg whites. Chill.

7   Melt the chocolate for the sauce in the liquid coffee.

8   Put a tbsp of the sauce on each place and top with the mousse.

CARAMELIZED JAPANESE PEAR GRATIN WITH WHITE CHOCOLATE SHAVINGS

SEE PAGE 114

INGREDIENTS

Sponge cake. For the cream: 2 leaves gelatine, 1/2 cup pureed Japanese pear juice, 1/4 cup fresh cream, 4 egg yolks, 1 tbsp sugar, 1 tbsp flour. For the meringue: 1/4 cup sugar, 1 tsp glucose, 1/4 cup water, 4 egg whites. For the filling: 3 Japanese pears, 1/4 cup white chocolate shavings. Garnish: 1 tbsp brown sugar, 4 scoops vanilla ice cream, crushed pistachio nuts, raspberry puree. For Poire William sabayon: 3 tbsps Poire William, 1 tsp sugar, 2 eggs.

SPECIAL EQUIPMENT

4 pastry rings

METHOD

1   Soak the gelatine. Bring the pear juice and cream to the boil. Mix the egg yolks with the sugar and flour and fold this into the hot pear juice and cream. Add the soaked gelatine.

2   Make the meringue by mixing together the sugar with the glucose and water and heat to the hard-ball stage.

3   Beat the egg whites and when stiff carefully fold in the hot sugar mixture. When well blended, fold into the pear pastry cream.

4   Poach the Japanese pears in sugar water until soft.

5   Line the bottom of the pastry rings with a very thin layer of sponge cake. Add a very thin slice of pear from one of the poached fruit, and a 1/4 of the white chocolate shavings. Top up with the pastry cream. Flatten and freeze.

6   Prepare the sabayon just before serving by mixing the Poire William, sugar and eggs together in a double boiler or a bowl set in hot water.

7   Sprinkle brown sugar on the top of each frozen dessert and caramelize under a hot grill. Serve immediately with vanilla ice cream, Poire William sabayon, raspberry puree, half a poached pear and a scattering of crushed pistachio nuts.

SWEET BABY BANANA PUDDING WITH ROASTED PINEAPPLE

SEE PAGE 115

INGREDIENTS

2 tbsps butter, 1/4 cup sugar, 2 egg yolks, 3/4 cup banana puree, juice of 1 lemon, 1 oz bitter chocolate, 1 tsp cornstarch, 1/4 cup ground roasted almonds. For the meringue: 2 egg whites, 2 tbsps sugar. Garnish: Roasted pineapple, chocolate wafers, and strawberry quarters.

EQUIPMENT

4 small or 1 large spring mould

METHOD

1   Cream the butter with the sugar. Add the egg yolks, banana puree and lemon juice.

2   Melt the chocolate in a double boiler. Add this to the banana mixture, together with the cornstarch and ground roasted almonds.

3   Beat the egg whites until thick. Fold in the sugar and continue beating until stiff.

4   Fold the egg whites lightly into the chocolate banana mixture.

5   Butter the spring mould(s) lightly and coat sparingly with sugar. Pour the prepared mixture into the moulds until approximately 3/4 full. Bake for 12 minutes at gas mark 7, 425° in a bain marie in the oven.

6   Serve with roasted pineapple, chocolate wafers and strawberry quarters.

ROASTED PINEAPPLE

Peel a ripe pineapple, slice and remove core. Pan fry the slices with butter and sugar in a non-stick pan until golden brown. Remove and cut into wedges.

INDEX

BEEF

Cilantro Encrusted, with Mushrooms and Wok Fried
Bell Peppers, 93
Japanese Beef Udon Noodle Soup, 35
Kobe, with Medley of Asian Vegetables, 105
Tagliatelle with Szechuan Sauce and Teppanyaki Sirloin, 49

CHICKEN

Chicken Breast, Honey Smoked, with
Contemporary Kim Chee, 104
Chicken Breast with Bak Choi and Baked Potatoes, 105
Silk Chicken Curry with Naan Bread, 104
Turmeric Chicken with Chili Flake Potato Salad, 17

CHOCOLATE

Cinnamon Chocolate Sandwich, 109
Caramelized Japanese Pear Gratin with
White Chocolate Shavings, 120
Five Spice Chocolate Mousse, 119
Sweet Baby Banana Pudding with Roasted Pineapple, 120
Sweet Gingered Teardrop with Cherries, 119

CRAB

Crab Cakes, Vietnamese, with Chili and Mustard, 75
Crab Claws with Black Bean Salad, 30
Crab Meat Salad, with Tangerine, on a Bed of
Marinated Tomatoes, 30

CRAYFISH:

Crayfish with Stir Fried Endive Salad and Basil, 31

DESSERT

Caramelized Japanese Pear Gratin
with White Chocolate Shavings, 120
Cinnamon Chocolate Sandwich, 109
Five Spice Chocolate Mousse, 119
Green Tea Souffle with Crystallized Oranges, 118
Hot Kaffir Lime Tart with Ginseng Ice Cream, 118
Sweet Baby Banana Pudding with Roasted Pineapple, 120
Sweet Gingered Teardrop with Cherries, 119
Thai Melon Medley, 117

DUCK

Duck Breast, Rose Liqueur Glazed, with Bouquet of
Greens, 103

FISH

Baby Turbot with Garlic, Basil and a Red Bean Sauce, 84
Garoupa, Steamed, with Lime and Green Onion, 86
Mackerel, Bronze Fennel Flavored, with Watercress,
and Satsuma Salad, 28
Monk Fish, Roasted, with Basil and Curry Sauce, 73
Mullet, Saffron with Siamese Tomato Risotto, 59
Salmon and Scallop Tartar, Wasabi Infused,
with Pickled Ginger, 31
Salmon, Cardamon Steamed, on Long Bean Salad, 83
Salmon, Crispy, with Saffron Pepper Jus, 87
Sole Fillet with Fire Roasted Mushrooms in a Lime
Turmeric Sauce, 84
Tuna Sashimi with Mizuna and Avocado, 29

LAMB

Baby Lamb Marinated with Sesame Oil,
Red Curry and Mint, 101
Lamb Carpaccio with Mustard, Curry and
Crushed Pepper, 27
Lamb Sauce, 101
Mongolian Lamb Shank with Ginger Flavored
Vegetables, 103

LOBSTER

Lobster, Sake Glazed, with Hot Japanese Vermicelli
and Cucumber Salad, 28
Lobster, Soya Steamed, with Snake Beans, 85

MISCELLANEOUS

Asian Pesto, 61
Crystallized Oranges, 118
Ginseng Ice Cream, 118
Naan Bread, 104
Roasted Pineapple, 120

PASTA

Beetroot Dim Sum with Asian Pesto, 60
Black Pepper Linguini with Red Tomato Sauce
and Bak Choi Stems, 58
Buckwheat Noodles with Bak Choi
and Fried Wild Garlic, 58
Chinese Ham and Anise Basil with Fettucine, 61
Cilantro-Seed Pasta Baked with Soya Yoghurt, 57
Hot Japanese Vermicelli and Cucumber Salad with Sake
Glazed Lobster, 28

Siamese Tomato Risotto with Saffron Mullet, 59
Soba Noodles with Green Mustard Leaves and Tofu, 68
Tagliatelle with Szechuan Sauce and Teppanyaki
Sirloin, 49
Thai Zucchini Lasagne with Kaffir Lime, 59

PHEASANT
Stir Fried Shell Pasta with Spinach and Pheasant, 60

PIGEON
Pigeon, Cayenne Pepper Glazed, with Bamboo Shoots, 102
Pigeon with Teppanyaki Vegetables and Herb Pesto, 91

PORK
Pork, Barbecued, 32
Pork, Barbecued Baby, with Curried Bean Salad, 29

SALADS/STARTERS
Ahi Tuna Sashimi with Mizuna and Avocado, 29
Barbecued Baby Pork with Curried Bean Salad, 29
Black Bean Salad with Crispy Sesame Crab Claws, 30
Bronze Fennel Flavored Mackerel with Watercress
and Satsuma Salad, 28
Chili Flake Potato Salad with Turmeric Chicken, 17
Hot Japanese Vermicelli and Cucumber Salad with
Sake Glazed Lobster, 28
Lamb Carpaccio with Mustard, Curry and Crushed
Pepper, 27
Stir Fried Endive Salad with River Crayfish and Basil, 31
Tangerine Crab Meat Salad on a Bed of Marinated
Tomatoes, 30
Wasabi Infused Tartar of Salmon and Scallops
with Pickled Ginger, 31

SALMON
Cardamom Steamed Salmon on Long Bean Salad, 83
Crispy Salmon with Saffron Pepper Jus, 87
Salmon and Scallop Tartar, Wasabi Infused,
with Pickled Ginger, 31

SCALLOPS
Roasted Scallop and Curry Soup with Sticky Rice, 45
Scallops, Sesame Crusted, on Red Chinese Spinach
Leaves, 85
Scallop and Salmon Tartar, Wasabi Infused,
with Pickled Ginger, 31

SEAFOOD
Choi Sum with Sweet Potatoes and an Egg White
Abalone Crust, 86
Crayfish with Stir Fried Endive Salad and Basil, 31

SOUPS
Dhal Soup with Barley and Shiso Tempura, 46
Gingered Tomato Broth with Celery Leaves, 46
Green Tea Soup with Chrysanthemum Petals, 44
Grilled Shiitake Mushroom Cappuccino with
Chili Powder, 43
Japanese Beef Udon Noodle Soup, 35
Lemon Leaf Bisque with Crisp Potato Matchsticks, 44
Roasted Scallop and Curry Soup with Sticky Rice, 45
Vietnamese Basil Soup with Lettuce and Prawns, 45

TOFU
Tofu, with Sweet and Sour Wok-Cooked Vegetables, 68
Tofu, with Soba Noodles and Green Mustard Leaves, 68

VEAL
Oriental Spiced Veal Cutlet, 102

VEGETARIAN
Broccoli with Honey and Mustard Sauce, 68
Camphor-Smoked Asparagus with Roasted Red Peppers, 69
Soba Noodles with Green Mustard Leaves and Tofu, 68
Sweet and Sour Wok-Cooked Vegetables with Tofu, 68
Wok- Fried Cantonese Vegetables with White Radish, 69